500
Five Minute Games

P9-CFN-516

3 9042 07738309 6

5/08

Other books by Jackie Silberg available from
Gryphon House

Games to Play With Babies

Games to Play With Toddlers

Games to Play With Two Year Olds

500
Five Minute Games

Quick and Easy Activities For 3-6 Year Olds

By Jackie Silberg

Illustrated by Rebecca Jones

gryphon house

Beltsville, Maryland USA

Acknowledgments

I want to thank the many parents, teachers and children who have played games with me and inspired the writing of my books.

A very special thank you to my editor, Kathy Charner, who has great imagination and insight and constantly encourages me. This is my fourth book with Kathy and I look forward to many more.

And, finally, to Larry and Leah Rood of Gryphon House. They believe in my work and treat me like a member of their own family. The care and concern that they have for young children is a constant reminder to me of how important our work is.

Copyright @ 1995 Jackie Silberg
Published by Gryphon House, Inc.
10726 Tucker Street, Beltsville MD 20705

Cover Design. Lightbourne Images
Illustrations: Rebecca Jones

Library of Congress Cataloging-in-Publication Data
  Silberg, Jackie, 1934-
    500 five minute games : quick and easy activities for 3-6 year
olds / by Jackie Silberg : illustrations by Rebecca Jones.
    P. cm.
  Includes index.
  ISBN13: 978-0-87659-172-7
  ISBN10: 0-87659-172-1
  1. Education games. 2. Early childhood education-Activity
  programs. 3. Motor ability in children, I. Title.
GVI480.S55 1995
790.1'922-dc20   95-7019
CIP

Table of Contents

Active Games   21

If you are looking for games in specific skills areas, see the Skills Index beginning on page 261.

Table of Contents

Table of Contents

Birthday Games   69

Table of Contents

Table of Contents

Drama Games   93

Table of Contents

Table of Contents

Language Games   121

Table of Contents

Listening Games   148

Table of Contents

Math Games   158

Table of Contents

Music Games   171

Table of Contents

Nursery Rhyme Games   193

Table of Contents

Relaxing Games   206

Rhyming Games   213

Table of Contents

Science Games   218

Table of Contents

Thinking Games   232

Transition Games   242

Table of Contents

Weather Games   248

Skills Index   261

Terms Index   268

Snickerdoodles

Teaches Body Awareness

- Play this game anytime, anywhere.
- Arrange the children in pairs.
- Name a part of the body.
- The children in each pair touch those parts together. For example, if the part of the body is "toes," each partner places his toes next to the other child's toes so that they touch.
- After naming a few parts of the body, say "snickerdoodles," and everyone changes partners.

Back to Back

Develops Body Awareness

- The children find a partner and stand facing each other.
- Recite the following chant.

    Hand to hand,

    Boom ti ada boom, boom.

    Hand to hand,

    Boom ti ada boom, boom.

- As the children say the chant, they open their hands and touch palm to palm.
- Repeat the chant, naming a different part of the body.

    Finger to finger...

    Boom ti ada boom, boom.

    Finger to finger...

    Boom ti ada boom, boom.

    Nose to nose...

- Make it more complicated by naming two parts of the body.
- Partners must touch one part to another, such as:

    Elbow to knee...

    Wrist to ankle...

    Back to back...

Active Games

Roll the Exercise

Improves Coordination

- Talk about the different kinds of exercise that the children like to do.
- Decide on three different exercises, for example, running in place, jumping jacks and touching toes.
- Sit in a circle and roll a ball to one of the children.
- This child chooses an exercise for everyone to do.
- After you have done the exercise, let the child who selected it roll the ball to another child.
- The game can continue for a long or short time.

Silly Moves

Teaches Body Awareness

- This activity gives young children an opportunity to practice identifying parts of their bodies.
- Ask the children to point to their noses.
- Ask them to point to their wrists.
- Then ask them to touch their noses to their wrists.
- The idea of the game is to touch one part of the body to another.
- Here are some movements that children love.

    Touch your elbow to your knee

    Touch your nose to your toe

    Touch your head to your leg

- Let the children invent their own movements.

Watch My Hand

Promotes Visual Skills

- Discuss all the different movements your hands can make.
- You can clap, snap, wave, shake and pound your fists together.
- Ask the children to watch and to copy what your hands do.
- Clap several times, then switch to another hand movement.
- Play the same game with feet and mouth movements.
- After the children have learned the game, let a child be the leader.

Rocking Fun

Teaches Coordination

- Ask each child to find a partner and sit on the floor facing his partner.
- Tell the children to sit with their legs crossed, holding their partner's hands.
- As the children say the popular rhyme "Miss Mary Mack," they rock back and forth.
- Start out slowly and go faster and faster.

Miss Mary Mack, Mack, Mack
All dressed in black, black, black
With silver buttons, buttons, buttons
Up and down her back, back, back.

Active Games

You Can Do It!

- If the children are getting a bit wiggly, this game will get out the wiggles.
- Ask the children to watch you.
- Recite the following poem.

    One, two, see what I can do.

    Copy me, and you can do it, too.

- Jump, hop, shake your hips, etc.
- Tell the children to imitate you.
- Choose a child to be the leader.

    Everyone repeats the two-line poem, and the child who is the leader picks a new movement to copy.

Wind Movements

Develops Creative Movement

- Talk about how the wind blows many things.
- Ask the children to name things blown by the wind.
- Have the children pretend to:

    Be leaves and flutter to the ground slowly.

    Be leaves blowing across the yard quickly.

    Be raindrops falling to the earth.

    Be feathers blown by the wind.

    Be snowflakes blown by the wind.

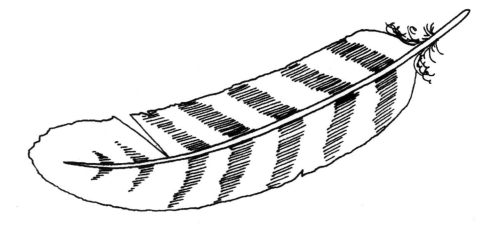

Moving High and Low

Teaches About High And Low

- The fluttering movement of a scarf helps to reinforce the concepts of high and low.
- Select one child to run around the room holding the scarf high in the air.
- As he runs, he raises and lowers his arm to experience the concepts of high and low.
- Making this kind of movement really helps a child internalize the concepts of high and low.
- Repeat with another child.

Speak With Your Body

Teaches Body Awareness

- Talk with the children about saying "yes" and "no."
- Explain to them that you are going to play a game in which they will answer yes and no with different parts of their bodies.
- Practice saying yes and no with your arms, shoulders, hips, toes, etc.
- Ask a question like "Do you like pizza?"
- Ask them to answer with their elbows.
- This game is good practice for remembering parts of the body and for exercising muscles.

Waving with Emotion

Improves Coordination

- Tell the children that they are going to practice waving.
- Everyone waves their hands in the air for a few seconds.
- Pretend that you are leaving home to go to school.
- Wave goodbye to your family.
- Other ways to wave include fast, slowly, vigorously, happily, sadly and with other parts of the body.

Active Games

Dancing Elbows

Develops Imagination

- Find a box large enough to hold a child.
- Cut two large holes in the box.
- One child gets into the box.
- Tell her to stick her elbows through the holes.
- Play music or ask the rest of the children to sing as the child inside the box moves her elbows to the music.
- Children always think this is very funny and enjoy seeing elbows dancing to the music.
- Repeat with another part of the body like feet, hands, head, etc.

One, Two, Three, Shape

Teaches Thinking Skills

- This excellent movement game requires a lot of thinking.
- Talk with the children about the shape of a circle.
- How could a body make a circle?
- If the children don't volunteer ideas, show them how to scrunch up into a ball, one way to make a circle.
- Now talk about the shape of a triangle.
- How could a body make a triangle?
- Lie on the floor with legs apart and arms down to your sides.
- Repeat with other shapes.
- Play the game, counting one, two, three, and naming a shape.
- The children try to make their bodies into that shape.

Body Movements

Improves Observation Skills

- Play a follow-the-leader game with the children.
- Ask the children to watch very carefully as you move different parts of your body.
- The children then imitate your movements.
- Make each movement four or five times before changing to the next movement.
- Try nodding your head, lifting your shoulders up and down, sticking out your tongue, shaking your hips, swinging your arms back and forth, etc.

Copy the Movements

Teaches Coordination

- Make a movement and ask the children to copy it. For example, kick your leg in the air.
- Make a second movement and ask the children to copy you again. This time, flap your arms like wings.
- Combine the two movements and ask the children to copy you.
- This game is an excellent sequencing activity.
- Add as many movements as the children can remember.

Moving Statues

Teaches Body Awareness

- Explain what a statue is.
- Ask the children to make themselves into statues.
- Ask them to move the statue across the room without changing its shape.
- Ask them to turn the statue around in a circle without changing shape.
- Ask them to move the statue very slowly, then very quickly, retaining its shape.
- Ask the children to make the statue FREEZE!

Active Games

At Our School

- Gather the children in a circle.
- Choose one child to perform actions inside the circle.
- Recite the following poem.

   At our school there is a boy,

   And every single day,

   He hop, hop, hops around the school

   While on the drum he plays.

- The chosen child hops around inside the circle, pretending to play a drum.
- Choose another child and repeat the poem.
- Keep the same instrument or substitute a different one.

A Movement Game

- This is a good activity for releasing energy.
- Begin this poem while sitting on chairs.

   Two little feet go tap, tap, tap.

   Two little hands go clap, clap, clap.

   One little child jumps up from the chair.

   Two little arms go up in the air.

   Two little hands go thump, thump, thump.

   Two little feet go jump, jump, jump.

   One little body turns around.

   One little child sits quietly down.

The Little Toad

Develops Coordination

- Recite the poem and perform the actions.

    I am a little toad,

    Hopping down the road. (hop fingers)

    Just listen to my song,

    I sleep all winter long. (pretend to be sleeping)

    When spring comes, I peep out,

    And then I jump about. (move arms around)

    And now I catch a fly, (pretend to catch something)

    And now I wink my eye, (wink one eye)

    And now and then I hop, (hop around)

    And now and then I stop. (stop hopping)

I Use My Brain

Enhances Body Awareness

- This wonderful movement poem helps children learn about the parts of their bodies.

    I use my brain to think, think, think. (touch head)

    I use my nose to smell. (touch nose)

    I use my eyes to blink, blink, blink. (touch eyes)

    I use my throat to yell. (touch throat and yell on word "yell")

    I use my mouth to giggle, giggle, giggle. (touch mouth)

    I use my hips to bump. (touch hips)

    I use my toes to wiggle, wiggle, wiggle. (touch toes)

    And I use my legs to jump. (jump)

    By Jackie Silberg

Active Games

Teddy Bear

Improves Coordination

- This popular children's rhyme is good for quick exercise.
- Recite the poem and perform the actions.

    Teddy bear, teddy bear, turn around.

    Teddy bear, teddy bear, touch the ground.

    Teddy bear, teddy bear, climb the stairs.

    Teddy bear, teddy bear, say your prayers.

    Teddy bear, teddy bear, turn out the light.

    Teddy bear, teddy bear, say "Goodnight."

Ring-Around-the-Rosy

Promotes Fun

- Children join hands and walk around in a circle.

    Ring-around-the-rosy,

    A pocketful of posies,

    Ashes, ashes,

    We all fall down. (fall to the ground)

- Recite the next verse while sitting on the floor.

    Penny on the water,

    Penny on the sea,

    Up jumps the little fish,

    And up jumps me. (jump up and repeat the game)

- Here is another verse to be said while sitting.

    Cows in the meadow,

    Eating buttercups,

    Ashes, ashes,

    We all jump up. (jump up and start again)

Pass the Ball

Encourages Cooperation

- Line the children up, one behind the other.
- Give the first child a ball.
- The object of the game is for the children to pass the ball through their legs to the back of the line.
- When the ball reaches the last person, she starts passing it forward over her head.
- The fun of the game is to see how fast the children can pass the ball.
- Say "Ready, set, go" and start counting.
- Each time they repeat the game, the children try to pass the ball faster.
- This game works best with older children.

Tightrope Walker

Teaches Balance

- Talk with the children about the circus.
- Ask them if they have ever seen a tightrope walker.
- Place a long strip of masking tape across the floor.
- Tell the children to pretend that this is a tightrope.
- Show the children how to walk very carefully on the tightrope, placing one foot in front of the other.
- Play instrumental music and let the children pretend to walk the tightrope.
- While they are walking, suggest other movements like balancing on one foot or walking backwards.

Active Games

Quick, Healthy Exercise

- Try the following exercises with the children.

    Deep Breathing—Show the children how to inhale and exhale. Practice a few times, then count to two slowly as they inhale and count to two slowly again as they exhale. This will help them develop a nice rhythm.

    Running in Place—Count to twenty-five as the children run in place.

    Jumping Jacks—Teach the children to do jumping jacks. Jump and extend your legs apart, then jump and bring your legs together. After they can do this, add the arm movements.

- All these exercises relieve stress and build healthy bodies at the same time.

Ankle Walk

Improves Coordination

- Line the children up on one side of the room.
- Ask them to bend over and hold onto their ankles.
- Have them walk to the other side of the room while holding onto their ankles.

Active Games

Shake It Up

Teaches Body Awareness

- Have the children identify different parts of their bodies and shake that part.
- They can shake their heads, hands, feet, toes, etc.
- This movement game helps develop coordination and cognitive skills as well.

Jogging

Teaches About Exercise

- Help the children become aware of their heart rate.
- Show them how to find their heartbeat and listen to how fast it is.
- On the word "go," tell the children to jog in place until you say "stop."
- Jog for fifteen to twenty seconds.
- Help them observe how much faster their heartbeat is after jogging.
- Explain to the children that jogging is healthy because it helps the heart exercise.

Hopping Fun

Improves Coordination

- Try this movement game to work out excess energy and develop coordination at the same time.
- Give the children an action word like "hop."
- Ask them to think of all the things that can hop, for example, rabbits, kangaroos and grasshoppers.
- Let one child at a time choose a thing that hops and demonstrate how it moves. Then ask the rest of the children to copy him.
- Other action words are run, jump, roll and slither.

Active Games

March in the Room

Improves Coordination

- Line the children up.
- March in different patterns around the room.
- March in a circle, diagonally across the room, in and out of tables, etc.
- Try marching backwards.
- Try other patterned movements.

Space Dance

Teaches About Forward And Backward

- Dancing is a wonderful way to introduce children to spatial concepts.
- Play instrumental music and ask the children to dance to the music in different ways.
- First move forward, then backwards. Do this several times before going to the next concept.
- Dance toward the window and away from the window.
- As the children dance, suggest different movements like marching, tiptoeing and gliding.
- Dance all around the room and then through the room.
- These concepts are a little harder to grasp and may take awhile.
- This game is more successful with older children.

Moving Fast and Slow

Teaches About Fast And Slow

- Play slow music.
- Encourage the children to move to the music by taking huge, soft giant steps.
- Another way to move very slowly is to sway like a branch blowing in the breeze.
- For a faster movement, play brisk music and suggest hopping in place, running on tiptoes or moving arms rapidly.
- This game helps children acquire the concepts of fast and slow.

Drumbeats

Enhances Listening Skills

- Beat a tom-tom or a hand drum rhythmically, asking the children to walk in time with the drumbeats.
- Beat the drum very slowly and ask them to walk very slowly.
- Beat the drum very fast and ask them to walk fast.
- Beat the drum loudly and ask them to take giant steps.
- Beat the drum softly and ask them to take tiny baby steps.
- Children who are four or five are able to walk to the actual beat. Three year olds have a harder time.
- Let the children take turns beating the drum fast and slow, loud and soft.

Be a Chair

Enhances Thinking Skills

- Set a chair where all the children can see it.
- Demonstrate how to fit your body into the shape of the chair.
- Bend your knees and fit your arms along the back of the chair.
- Ask the children to copy you.
- Now ask the children to walk around the room, keeping their bodies in the shape of the chair.
- Try molding your body into other shapes like a shoe, a dress or a hat.
- Try flattening your body and moving around while keeping as flat as possible.

Active Games

Air Games

Teaches About Spatial Relationships

- When the children need to get rid of excess energy, try this game.
- Suggest that they:

    Hit the air

    Punch the air

    Kick the air

    Hug the air

    Pat the air

    Brush the air

    Push the air

    Throw the air

    Catch the air

- Perform these actions fast, slowly, softly or hard.

Jack-in-the-Box

Improves Coordination

- The children crouch down while reciting the first three lines of the rhyme in very soft voices.
- On the last line, they jump up and say, "Yes, I will!" in big voices.

    Jack-in-the-box

    Sits so still.

    Won't you come out?

    "Yes, I will!"

Body Crayons

Develops Creativity

- Ask the children to pretend that their bodies are crayons.
- Let them tell you what color crayon they would like to be.
- The "paper" for drawing is the floor.
- Suggest that they use their bodies to draw all over the paper.
- Here are some suggestions for them.

    Scribble all over the paper.

    Draw big lines and little lines.

    Draw long lines and short lines.

    Draw small circles.

Open and Close

Teaches Body Awareness

- Children enjoy the popular rhyme "Open, Shut Them."

    Open, shut them, open, shut them,

    Give a little clap.

    Open, shut them, open, shut them,

    Put them in your lap.

- Ask the children what other parts of the body can open and shut. As the children name other parts of the body, experiment to see whether they will open and shut.
- Try arms, shoulders, eyes, mouth, etc.

Active Games

Moving in Space

- Ask the children to move around the room in different ways.

    Walk slowly and softly

    Walk fast and softly

    Jump low

    March backwards

    Walk like a robot

    Hop on one foot with arms out straight

- This game can go on for as long as you want it to.

Be a Machine

Encourages Imagination

- Talk about machines in the house, like the washing machine, the toaster, the vacuum cleaner, the clock, etc.
- The first time that you play this game, choose two or three machines that the children can pretend to be, perhaps a clock and a vacuum cleaner.
- Talk about how these machines work.
- Help the children pretend to be a clock or a vacuum cleaner.
- When you say, "Machines go!" the children begin pretending.
- When you say, "Machines stop!" they stop.
- As you play this game, you will discover that the children invent many ideas themselves.

Watch the Body

Promotes Observation Skills

- Invite one child to come to the front of the room and stand still.
- Whispering to her, ask her to move one part of her body.
- She should move that part (arm, leg, etc.) very, very slightly, then stand perfectly still again.
- The children have to watch very attentively to see which part of the body moves.

Stay in Place

Teaches Body Awareness

- Give each child a piece of masking tape to place on the floor.
- Ask them to stand on the tape and move their bodies without moving their legs.
- Experiment by moving arms, necks, heads, mouths and hips.
- Play instrumental music while the children move.

Alphabet Games

The Mix-up

- Draw a circle, a square and a triangle.
- Place letters inside each of the shapes.
- Two letters inside each shape is a good start. For example, place the letter "T" and the letter "M" inside the circle.
- Now ask the children a variety of questions.

    What shape contains the letter "T"?

    Inside what shape is the letter "M" etc.?

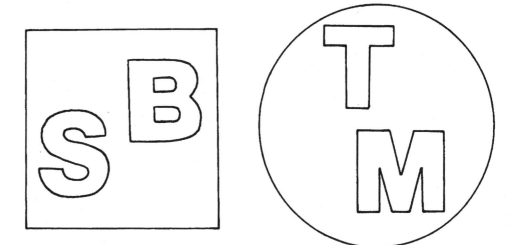

Hot Letters

- This is a variation of the game "Hot Potato."
- Sit the children in a circle and pass out cards with one letter on each card.
- Tell the children that you are going to play music.
- Ask them to pass their cards around the circle while the music is playing.
- Ask them to stop passing the cards when the music stops.
- Be sure to practice the direction in which they should pass the cards.
- Play the game, and when the music stops, ask each child to name the letter on his card.
- Play this game for number, shape and color recognition.

Alphabet Games

The ABC Song

Encourages Listening Skills

- Choose one child.
- Ask him to say the letter with which his name begins, out loud.
- Sing the ABC song, and when you come to that letter in the alphabet, pause long enough to say the letter silently, then continue with the next letter.
- For example, if the child's name is Jonathan, say "A B C D E F G H I _ K L M N O P, etc.
- Great fun!

Alphabet Game

Improves Listening Skills

- Children know and enjoy singing the "ABC" song.
- Make alphabet cards in advance and give one card to each child.
- Instruct the children to hold up their letter as it is sung.
- Sing the song very slowly, to enable the children to hear and hold up their letter.
- To simplify the activity, line the children up in order, from A to Z.
- If you have more cards than children, give some children two cards.

What's on My Back?

Develops Concentration

- Use your finger to draw one letter on a child's back.
- See if she can guess the name of the letter.
- Draw the same letter on another child's back.
- Encourage the children to draw letters on each other's backs.
- With older children, draw their names on their backs.

Alphabet Games

Following the Alphabet

- Give each child a card with one letter of the alphabet on it.
- Ask the "A" cardholder to stand up so that the rest of the children can see her.
- Everyone says together,

    "Letter A, letter A, what comes next?"
- The "B" cardholder now stands up, and everyone says together,

    "Letter B, letter B, what comes next?"
- Continue until the children have named all of the letters.

Same Sounds

Teaches Alliteration

- Make up sentences using words that start with the same sound.
- Begin each sentence with a child's name.

    Mary's mommy made macaroons.

    Susan sang a silly song.

    Brett brought me some bread.
- This will be hard to do with some names.
- Pick names with initial sounds that are easy to hear.

42

Alphabet Games

Listen to the Letter

- Ask one child to say her name.
- Then ask the other children if they can think of another word that begins with the same sound.
- On a piece of paper, a chalkboard or an easel, write the child's name and, under the name, the suggested words.
- Look at the list with the children.
- Compare the sounds.
- The children will be able to match letters, even if they don't know a particular word.

Sing, Alphabet, Sing

Teaches Sound Awareness

- Divide the group into four parts.
- Discuss different ways to sing: loud, soft, high, low, fast, slow, whisper, etc.
- Let each group choose which kind of voice they want to use.
- Each group sings parts of the alphabet song in different voices.
- Sing the alphabet song.

    Part 1—ABCDEFG

    Part 2—HIJKLMNOP

    Part 3—QRSTUV

    Part 4—WXYZ

- Everyone sing together.

    Now I've said my ABC's

    Next time won't you sing with me.

Alphabet Games

Walk Around the Letter

Teaches Letter Recognition

- Put masking tape on the floor in the shape of the letter "D."
- With the children, say the letter and think of "D" words.
- Point out to the children that the letter "D" has a round part and a straight part.
- Walk around the letter and sing this song to the tune of "London Bridge Is Falling Down."

  Walk around the letter D, letter D, letter D,

  Walk around the letter D,

  My fair lady.

- Try this game with other letters.

Naming Words

Enhances Thinking Skills

- Put cards with letters on them (one letter per card) in a basket.
- One child selects a card from the basket.
- Ask the child to name the letter that she selected and something that starts with this letter.
- Challenge the older children by asking them to name other words that start with the same letter.
- Younger children will need help with this game.

Jump for Joy

Practices Letter Recognition

- Prepare cards with one letter of the alphabet on each card.
- Show the children the card with the letter "J."
- Tell them to jump every time that they see the letter "J."
- Show them a card with the word "Jump" written on it, so that they can see that "Jump" starts with "J."
- Hold up one alphabet card at a time.
- Insert the letter "J" about every three or four cards.
- Play this game using another letter such as "G" for gallop, "S" for sit, "H" for hop and so on.

Fuzzy Wuzzy Caterpillar

Teaches About Butterflies

- This is a nice poem that helps children understand how a caterpillar changes into a butterfly.

    Fuzzy wuzzy caterpillar,

    Into a corner crept.

    Spun around himself a blanket,

    And for a long time slept. (curl up and pretend to sleep)

    Roly-poly caterpillar,

    Wakening by and by,

    Found himself with beautiful wings,

    Changed to a butterfly. (fly around the room with arms spread)

The Turtle

Teaches About Turtles

- This fingerplay is fun to do and teaches children how turtles can withdraw into their shells.

    This is a turtle. (make a fist with one hand)

    He lives in a shell.

    He likes his home,

    Very, very well.

    He pokes his head out when he wants something to eat,
        (stick thumb out from fist)

    And puts it back in when he goes to sleep.
        (fold thumb back into fist)

Animal Games

Houses

- Children will enjoy learning about where animals live while doing this fingerplay.

  Here is a nest for bluebirds. (cup hands together to make a nest)

  Here is a hive for bees. (interlock fingers to make a hive)

  Here is a hole for the bunny. (make a circle with index finger and thumb to make a hole)

  And here is a house for me! (touch fingertips together to make a roof)

Worms

- Young children are usually fascinated by worms.
- Consider following the poem with a discussion about why worms are important.

  Worms, worms,
  Worms crawling in the ground.
  Worms, worms,
  Worms crawling all around.

  Fat worms, thin worms,
  Wiggling, wiggling.
  Short worms, long worms,
  Squiggling, squiggling.

  Worms, worms,
  Worms crawling in the ground.
  Worms, worms,
  Worms crawling all around.

  If I was a wiggle, wiggle worm
  I would wiggle like this!! (wiggle like worms)

  By Jackie Silberg

If I Were a Bird

Teaches About Birds

- Recite the following poem and perform the actions.

    If I were a bird,

    I'd sing a song,

    And fly around the whole day long.
      (flap arms like the wings of a bird)

    When it was dark,

    I'd go to rest,

    In my cozy little nest.
      (cup hands together to make a nest)

Did You Ever See a Lassie?

Develops Coordination

- This popular children's song is fun to sing and act out.
- Substitute the name of an animal for "lassie" and move the way that the animal moves.

    Did you ever see a monkey, a monkey, a monkey,

    Did you ever see a monkey go this way and that?

    This way ... etc.

- Sing the song about an elephant, a bunny, a kangaroo, a bird, a dinosaur, etc.

Animal Games

A Different Old MacDonald

- Sing the familiar song "Old MacDonald Had a Farm" as usual, but at the end of each verse, ask the children what the animal named in that verse eats.
- For example, for the verse that begins "On his farm he had a cow," after the children sing "moo, moo," ask them what a cow eats.
- Continue singing the song, asking at the end of each verse about the animal named.

Animal Movements

- Tell the children that they are going to name an animal and try to move like that animal.
- Demonstrate to the children how a few animals move.
- For example, creep like a cat, slither like a snake, hop like a bunny, walk like an elephant or crawl like an ant.
- Name one animal at a time, and ask the children to act out its movement.

Follow Peter

Improves Coordination

- This is an enjoyable game to play at Easter.
- Choose someone to be Peter Rabbit. Peter is the leader, and everyone imitates what Peter does.
- Here are a few ideas for Peter.
    Wrinkle your nose
    Hop on one foot
    Hop on both feet
    Eat a carrot
- Sing "Here Comes Peter Cottontail."

Theme Songs

Enhances Creative Thinking

- Choose a subject and try to think of two or more songs about that subject.
- For example, sing two songs about animals such as "Five Little Ducks" and "Five Little Monkeys."
- Divide the children into two groups.
- One group sings "Five Little Ducks," and when they are finished, the other group sings "Five Little Monkeys."
- This is a fun way to rehearse the songs that you already know.

Animal Games

Magic Sounds

Improves Creativity

- Pretend to hold a magic wand.
- Tell the children that you are all going to sing "Old MacDonald Had a Farm," and that whoever is tapped on the shoulder by the magic wand will get to choose the animal and make that animal's sound.
- Sing the song, and when you reach the words "And on his farm he had a _____," tap a child on the shoulder.
- That child names an animal for that verse.
- During the next verse, the child will hold the magic wand and tap another child on the shoulder.

Pretending

Enhances Imagination

- Ask the children to lie down and be very still.
- Say the following words: "Abracadabra, I see a bear."
- Tell the children that when they hear the name of an animal, they can get up and pretend to be that animal.
- When the children hear the words "Abracadabra" again, that is their signal to lie down and listen for the next animal to be named.
- After they have learned to play the game, let the children decide what animals they would like to be.

Bunny Hopping

Improves Coordination

- Talk about all the ways that bunnies can hop.
- Move around the room like a bunny. Start with large leaps and short jumps.
- Let the children hop around the room to a specific place. Hop to the window or hop to the door.
- Suggest to the children other ways to hop.

    Hop quietly, so that no one will hear you

    Hop as if you are scared and want to get home quickly

    Hop and stop to sniff the vegetables

Busy Bees

Teaches Body Awareness

- Ask the children to move around the room saying "bzzz, bzzz, bzzz," pretending to be bees.
- Call out the name of a part of the body, like elbows.
- The children stop and touch their elbows gently to another child's elbow.

The Elephant Game

Promotes Cooperation

- Divide the children into groups of three.
- Explain to them that when you say the word "elephant," they should pretend to be different parts of an elephant.
- The child in the middle is the trunk. She bends at the waist and clasps her hands together, swinging them from side to side like a trunk.
- The two children on either side of the elephant trunk make ear shapes with their arms.
- As the elephant trunk swings, the ears flap back and forth.
- Play the game by pointing to a group of three children and saying the word "elephant."
- When you point to another group, the first group can stop.

Animal Games

Hopping

Improves Coordination

- Show the children how a grasshopper, a rabbit and a frog hop.
- Choose three children, one to be the grasshopper, one to be the rabbit and one to be the frog.
- As you recite the following poem, ask the three children to act it out while hopping in a circle.

    A grasshopper hopped up to the tree.

    He saw a frog and said, "Come hop with me."

    The frog and the grasshopper hopped to a tree,

    And saw a rabbit and said, "Come hop with me."

    They hopped and hopped all around and,

    Finally they stopped and fell down.

- Repeat the poem with three different children.

The Birds Can Fly

Develops Creative Thinking

- Call out the name of a bird that flies.
- Ask the children to flap their arms like wings.
- Call out the name of an animal that doesn't fly.
- Everyone stops flapping their wings.
- Name another bird that flies, and everyone starts flapping again.
- The idea of the game is to name several birds in a row and then to name an animal that does not fly.
- This is a lot of fun and an excellent way to teach listening skills.

Monkey See and Monkey Do

Teaches Body Awareness

- Recite the following poem.
- Ask the children to copy what you do.

  The monkey stamps his feet. (stamp your feet)

  The monkey stamps his feet. (children stamp their feet)

  Monkey see and monkey do,

  The monkey does the same as you.

- Explain to the children that one person is the leader, and everyone else is a monkey.
- The leader acts, and the monkeys copy the action.
- Repeat the poem with other actions like walking, clapping, jumping, swimming, etc.

Duck, Duck, Goose

Promotes Cooperation

- This very, very popular game never loses its magic.
- Seat the children in a circle and choose one child to be "it."
- That child walks around the circle and taps the others on the head, saying "duck."
- When she taps a child on the head and says "goose," that child gets up and runs around the circle trying to tag the child who is "it."
- If the child who is "it" sits down in the empty place before she is caught, the new child becomes "it."

Animal Games

Elephants

- Ask the children to form two lines facing each other.
- The children in one line are the elephants.
- The children in the other line are the greeters.
- Recite the poem.
- The children who are elephants perform the actions in the first two lines, and the children who are greeters perform the action in the fourth line.

  The elephant walks with great big feet. (bend over and walk like an elephant)

  Thump, thump, thump.

  He swings his trunk from side to side. (clasp hands together and swing them from side to side)

  When you greet him, shake his trunk up and down. (take the "trunks" and shake them up and down)

- Switch sides and let the elephants be the greeters; and the greeters become elephants.

Elephants and Kangaroos

- Divide the children into two groups, elephants and kangaroos.
- Elephants bend over at the waist and swing their arms from side to side. They take slow, lazy steps.
- Kangaroos put their feet together, their hands up with elbows bent, and they take small jumps across the room.
- Let the elephants start on one side and the kangaroos on the opposite side of the room.
- When the elephants reach the other side, ask them to lift their arms up in the air and give a loud elephant roar.

Slowly, Slowly

- The children act out the words of this chant.

    Slowly, slowly, very slowly,

    Creeps the garden snail.

    Slowly, slowly, very slowly,

    Up the wooden rail. (say the words very, very slowly)

    Quickly, quickly, very quickly,

    Creeps the little bug.

    Quickly, quickly, very quickly,

    Underneath the rug. (say the words very quickly)

The Animal in Me

Encourages Creative Thinking

- After a trip to the zoo or a reading of an animal picture book, let each child pick out a favorite animal.
- Ask the children to imitate the movements and sounds of the animal each has chosen.
- Start with one child at a time. Let the child name the animal and then imitate it.
- When all the children have had a turn, let them imitate all of the animals together.
- A good song to sing after this activity is "I Went to the Animal Fair."

Animal Games

This Little Cow Eats Grass

- Choose five children to be the cows.
- Talk about the different things that each cow does.
- One cow eats grass—this child pretends to eat grass.
- Another cow eats hay—this child pretends to eat hay.
- One cow drinks water—this child pretends to drink water from a pail.
- Another cow runs away—this child runs across the room.
- The fifth cow lies down all day—this child lies down on the floor. On the words "chase her, chase her," the fifth child gets up and runs across the room while all the other children chase her.

> *This little cow eats grass.*
>
> *This little cow eats hay.*
>
> *This little cow drinks water,*
>
> *And this little cow runs away.*
>
> *This little cow does nothing, but just lies down all day.*
>
> *We'll chase her, we'll chase her, we'll chase her away.*

The Bunny Game

- Choose a child to be the first bunny.
- Recite the following poem as that child hops around the room.
- On the line "Hop, he goes into the ground," the hopping bunny falls down.
- Choose another child to be the bunny.

> *This is the bunny (point to the bunny)*
>
> *With ears so funny. (pretend to have bunny ears)*
>
> *This is the hole in the ground. (point to the center of the circle)*
>
> *If a noise he hears, he pricks up his ears,*
>
> *And HOP, he goes into the ground.*

Hopping Rabbit

Teaches About Rabbits

- This is a good movement poem for releasing energy.

    I saw a little rabbit come hop, hop, hop. (hop around the room)

    I saw his little ears go flop, flop, flop. (pretend to flap bunny ears)

    I saw his little nose go twink, twink, twink. (wiggle your nose)

    I saw his little eyes go wink, wink, wink. (wink your eyes)

    I said, "Little Rabbit, won't you stay?"

    He looked at me and he hopped away. (hop around the room)

There Once Was a Sow

Teaches Counting Skills

- Designate one part of the room as the pigpen.
- Choose one child to be the pig and sit in the pigpen.
- This child says "umph" in the poem.

    There once was a sow who had a piglet,

    And a piglet had she.

    And the old sow always went "umph," (child says "umph")

    And the piglet went "wee, wee, wee." (another child goes to the pigpen and says "wee, wee, wee")

- Choose a different child to go to the pigpen.
- Repeat the poem.
- Children love this game and make the sounds with enthusiasm.

Animal Games

Hop Little Bunny

Develops Coordination

- Ask the children to form a line.
- The child at the head of the line is the "bunny" leader and can decide how the rest of the "bunnies" move through the garden, by jumping, skipping, turning, etc.
- The "bunnies" follow the leader as everyone recites the poem.

    Hop little bunny,

    Hop away free.

    Hop through the garden,

    Then come back to me.

- Choose a new "bunny" leader.

A Fishy Story

Develops Counting Skills

- Ask the children to form a circle.
- Choose one child to be the fish. He stands in the middle.
- Ask the fish to make a "fish face" while the rest of the children recite the following poem.

    1, 2, 3, 4, 5,

    I caught a fish alive.

    6, 7, 8, 9, 10,

    We let it go again.

- While you are saying "We let it go again," open up the circle and allow the fish to "swim" out.
- Choose another child to be the fish.

Counting Bunnies

Enhances Counting Skills

- This fingerplay develops hand-eye coordination as well as counting skills. And children love it!

    My bunnies now must go to bed, (hold up one hand with fingers extended)

    The little father rabbit said.

    But first I will count them just to see, (point to extended fingers)

    If my bunnies have all come back to me.

    One bunny, two bunnies, three bunnies dear, (point to each finger as you count them)

    Four bunnies, five bunnies ... yes, they all are here.

    You are the prettiest bunnies alive,

    My bunnies, one, two, three, four, five. (count each finger again)

Animal Fun

Develops Observation Skills

- Find large pictures of three animals.
- With one hand or a piece of paper, cover up part of one animal.
- Can the children identify the animal?
- If not, expose more of the animal until the children are able to name it.
- After they have identified it, cover up one part of the animal and ask the children to tell which part is hidden.

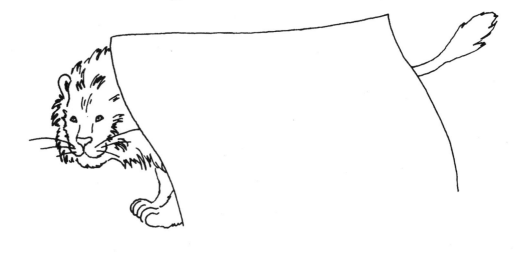

Animal Games

Imaginary Walk

Encourages Imagination

- Show the children how to go for an imaginary walk by tapping their hands on their thighs.
- Pretend to go on a walk to look for animals.
- Everyone taps their thighs.
- Go around the circle, and ask each child to name an animal that he sees on their imaginary walk.
- Before you play the game, it is a good idea to review the names of zoo animals, farm animals and pets.

Animal Stories

Teaches Speech Patterns

- Name an animal, and ask the children what sound the animal makes. For example, the children may tell you that a dog says "woof, woof."
- Using the words that the children give you, create a short chant.

    Dog, dog says, "Woof, woof, woof."

- Ask the children to repeat the chant.
- Practice saying the chant and clapping your hands in time with the words.
- Repeat the words and tap the rhythm on your head, on your knees, on your stomach, etc.
- This game develops the skill of listening to patterns in speech.

The Frozen Zoo

Improves Creative Thinking

- Ask the children what animal they would like to be, if they lived in the zoo.
- Ask them to show you how their animals would stand and how the faces of the animals would look.
- Set up a "frozen zoo."
- Each child (zoo animal) decides how she wants to look and freezes in place. For example, a monkey might swing from a rope, and a seal might swim in the water.
- Take a picture of the frozen zoo. The children will really enjoy seeing themselves.

Ride a Little Horsey

Encourages Fun

- Pretend to ride a horse.
- Hold onto the reins and recite the following poem.

    Ride a little horsey,

    Down to town.

    You better be careful,

    So you don't fall down.

- Everyone falls down on the last line.
- Repeat this poem very slowly and very fast.
- Great fun!!

Animal Names

Promotes Creative Thinking

- Ask each child to think of his favorite animal.
- Then ask each child to introduce himself as that animal.
- If Billy likes bears, he would say, "My name is Billy the Bear, and here is how I say hello." Billy would make a bear sound.

Animal Games

Special Statues

Encourages Creativity

- Choose one child to be the leader.
- The leader walks around the room with everyone following her.
- Suddenly, the leader turns around and names an animal, for example, "snakes."
- Everyone must freeze in position to look like snakes.
- The leader starts walking again, turns and says "frogs." Everyone must freeze to look like frogs.
- Choose another child to be the leader, either a few minutes into the game, or the next day.

The Farm

Improves Observation Skills

- Talk about the various animals that live on a farm.
- Encourage the children to make the sounds of different animals.
- Choose one child to be the farmer.
- Tell the rest of the children to pick their favorite farm animal.
- When you say "go," the children make the sound of that animal.
- While the children continue to make their sounds, ask the farmer to cover her eyes, because one animal will be going back into the barn.
- After the farmer's eyes are covered, ask one child to leave the area. Then ask the farmer to guess who is missing.

Little Blackbirds

Promotes Creativity

- This popular poem is great fun to act out. Choose two children to be the blackbirds.

    Two little blackbirds sitting on a hill, (flap arms like wings)

    One named Jack, (or substitute one child's name)

    And one named Jill. (or substitute the other child's name)

    Fly away Jack, (one child flies to a designated place)

    Fly away Jill. (the other child flies to a designated place)

    Come back Jack, (one child flies back)

    Come back Jill. (the other child flies back)

Bumblebee, Bumblebee

Teaches Thinking Skills

- Discuss with the children where a bumblebee could hide in the room: on the window sill, on the ceiling, in a drawer, etc.
- Choose one child to be the bumblebee.
- She decides but does not tell anyone where she is hiding.
- The children ask the bumblebee questions to discover where she is hiding.
- If the answer is no, the bumblebee says "bzzz, bzzz" while shaking her head "no."
- If the answer is yes, she buzzes all around the room and "lands" on another child. Whomever she touches, becomes the next bumblebee.

Animal Games

This Little Pig

Enhances Imagination

- Choose five children to be the little pigs.
- Talk about what each pig does in the poem.

    This little pig danced a merry, merry jig.

    This little pig ate candy.

    This little pig wore a blue and yellow wig.

    This little pig was a dandy.

    This little pig never grew very big,

    So they called him tiny little Andy.

- Create movements and actions for each of the little pigs.

    Danced a jig—make up jumping steps

    Ate candy—pretend to lick a lollipop

    Wore a wig—pretend to comb your hair

    Was a dandy—make funny faces

    Tiny little Andy—crawl on the floor

- Recite the poem.
- Choose five other children to play the game.

Hungry Bunny

Develops Creativity

- This is a nice poem to act out on a cold winter day.

    A funny little snowman

    Had a carrot nose.

    Along came a bunny,

    And what do you suppose?

    That bunny was very hungry

    And was looking for some lunch.

    He ate that little snowman's nose,

    Crunch, crunch, crunch.

- Let the children take turns being the bunny and the snowman.
- Pass out carrots to the children to eat at the sound of "crunch."

Little Mice

Promotes Creativity

- Gather the children together.
- Choose one child to be the big black cat.
- The rest of the children are the little mice.
- Recite the following poem.

    The little mice go creeping, creeping, creeping,

    The little mice go creeping,

    All through the house.

- The children pretend to be mice and creep slowly around the room. Suggest that they squeak and sniff.

    The big black cat comes stalking, stalking, stalking,

    The big black cat comes stalking,

    All through the house.

- The child who is the cat takes big steps and meows.

    The little mice all scamper, scamper, scamper,

    The little mice all scamper,

    All through the house.

- The mice run quickly and hide behind something. As they run, they whisper "scamper, scamper" in little mouse voices.

Lions and Lambs

Enhances Creativity

- Tell the children about the expression, "March comes in like a lion and goes out like a lamb."
- Talk about the differences between the two animals, how one is strong and forceful, while the other is gentle and quiet.
- Divide the class into two groups, the lions and the lambs.
- The lion's poem is:

    Ho, ho, ho, I'm the king of the jungle.

    Ho, ho, ho, I'm the ruler of the crowd.

    Ho, ho, ho, I'm the king of the jungle.

    Ho, ho, ho, I can roar scary loud.

Animal Games

Do what I tell you,
Do what I say,
Or I'll roar and I'll roar,
And I'll frighten you away!

By Jackie Silberg

- The lamb's poem is "Mary Had a Little Lamb."
- Repeat the expression, "March comes in like a lion."
- The "lions" act like lions while the lion poem is recited.
- Repeat "And goes out like a lamb."
- The "lambs" recite "Mary Had a Little Lamb" in soft, quiet voices.

Dog Talk

Develops Imagination

- Tell the children that they are going to pretend to be dogs. Encourage them to crawl on all fours and bark like dogs.
- Now tell them that the dogs have learned to speak English.
- Ask them to share with their classmates what life is like as a dog.
- Ask them "What did you have for breakfast?" or "What games did you play this morning?"
- Play the same game, choosing other animals.

Animal Games

Monkey Game

- Talk with the children about monkeys.
- Discuss all the things monkeys can do like climbing, swinging, hopping, jumping, etc.
- Ask the children to make monkey sounds.
- Invite one child at a time to show the rest of the children something a monkey would do.
- Call on children by using their first names and "Monkey" as their last name. For example, "Bianca Monkey, show us what monkeys do."
- Bianca performs the action, and the others imitate her.
- Continue with other children.

Groundhog

Teaches About Groundhog Day

- Choose one child to be the groundhog.
- She rolls herself into a ball and pretends to be inside a hole in the ground.
- Recite this poem with the children.

    Groundhog, groundhog, come on out and play.
    It's a beautiful, beautiful February day.
    The sun is shining and the sky is blue.
    Won't you come on out, we want to play with you.

    By Jackie Silberg

- The groundhog slowly comes out of the hole and looks around.
- She sees her shadow and says, "Oh, dear, there will be six more weeks of winter."
- Then the groundhog goes back inside her hole.
- Recite this poem with the children.

    Groundhog, groundhog, come on out and play.
    It's a gloomy, gloomy, February day.
    The air feels chilly and the sky is gray.
    Won't you come on out, we want to play today.

    By Jackie Silberg

- This time the groundhog comes out and says, "Okay, let's play. I don't see my shadow."

Animal Games

Walking to the Zoo

- Choose two children to start the game. One child is the pig.
- The children stand at opposite sides of the room and act out the following poem.
- Everyone speaks:

  As I was walking to the zoo one bright and sunny day,

  One pink pig passed me by, going the other way. (the child who is the pig should waddle across the room)

  "Oink, oink," said the pink pig.

  "Hello," said I.

  "Oink, oink," said the pink pig.

  Then we both said, "Goodbye."

- The two children walk to opposite sides of the room.
- Repeat the poem again, substituting a different animal.

Birthday Games

The Birthday

- Any birthday (or unbirthday) child will love this fingerplay.

    Billy (substitute any child's name) had a birthday,
    And Billy had a cake! (make a circle with arms)
    Billy's grandma made it, (stir the batter)
    And Billy watched it bake.

    Frosting on the top, (hold right hand out flat)
    Frosting in between. (place left hand under right hand)
    Oh, it was the nicest cake
    That you have ever seen!

    Billy had some candles,
    One, two, three, four, five. (hold fingers up one at a time)
    Who can tell me how many years
    Billy has been alive?

The Birthday Game

Encourages Listening Skills

- Young children love to talk about their birthdays.
- Choose one child.
- Everyone recites the poem. When they reach the birthday month of the chosen child, she stands up.
- Repeat the poem, and let another child have a turn.

    Apples, peaches, pears and plums,
    Tell me when your birthday comes.
    January, February, March, April, May, June, July, August,
    September, October, November, December.

Birthday Games

On My Birthday

Builds Memory Skills

- Children love to talk about their birthdays and about birthday presents. This game combines both of these loves.
- The first child says, "On my birthday I want a doll." The next child says, "On my birthday I want a doll and a tricycle." The next child repeats the phrase, adding a third item.
- This game is very challenging and also very funny.
- Sometimes the children laugh at the items suggested as birthday presents.
- They may also say funny things like "On my birthday I want a gorilla."
- Younger children may need help remembering what others have already said.

Billy Had a Little Lamb

Develops Social Skills

- Sing the song "Mary Had a Little Lamb."
- Choose one child and substitute his name for "Mary." If any child is celebrating a birthday, choose that child.
- Ask the children what they like about the chosen child, then sing about that attribute. For example,

    Billy had a little lamb,

    Little lamb, little lamb,

    Billy had a little lamb,

    And we like Billy's smile.

- You can also exchange the word "lamb" for something else.

Creative Cupcakes

Develops Creativity

- For a special treat, like a birthday or holiday, serve the children cupcakes with white icing.
- Set out an assortment of colored sprinkles and let them decorate their own cupcakes.
- Pass out red-hots, and let the children pretend that their cupcakes have the chicken pox.

The Birthday Train

Enhances Creative Thinking

- Ask the children to form a circle.
- Take the hand of one child.
- Walk around the inside of the circle with that child as everyone chants,

   Come aboard the birthday train,

   Come aboard the birthday train.

   What do you want for your birthday?

   Come aboard the birthday train.

- Pause in front of one child.
- Ask him to say what he wants for his birthday.
- After he does, ask him to join the train.
- Continue chanting the verse until all the children have had a turn to tell what they want for their birthday.
- As the game ends, there will be one large birthday train!

Birthday Games

Practicing Letter Sounds

Teaches Letter Recognition

- This game is a good way to honor a birthday child.
- Discuss with the children the letter with which the birthday child's name begins.
- Try to think of many words that start with the same sound.
- As the children say each word, write it down so they can see it.
- After you are finished, they will be able to see that all the words begin with the same letter.

Watch the Conductor

Practices Observation Skills

- Choose one child to be conductor of the "chorus" (the other children). If you have a birthday child, choose her.
- Show the conductor how to put her index fingers to her mouth to signal a soft sound, and how to hold her arms out straight and to the sides to signal a loud sound.
- Have the children sing a familiar song like "Twinkle, Twinkle, Little Star."
- Tell them to watch the conductor to know whether to sing loudly or softly.

Special Birthday Game

Develops Self-esteem

- Sing this song to the tune of "Are You Sleeping" to the birthday child.

  Happy Birthday, Happy Birthday,

  We like you, we like you.

  You are very special,

  You are very special.

  Hip, hooray,

  Hip, hooray.

- Ask each child to tell something special about the birthday child.
- Suggest that they start their sentence with "I like (child's name) because..."

Everybody Has a Birthday

Encourages Creative Thinking

- Talk with the children about what they like to do on their birthdays.
- Then say the following poem together.

    Everybody has a birthday.

    It's a special day when you were born.

    When you celebrate your birthday,

    There are many things that you can do.

    By Jackie Silberg

- Ask each child to tell the date of his birthday.
- Let each child tell one thing that he likes to do on his birthday.

Color Games

Think Blue

- Gather together pictures of things that are all of the same color, for example, blue.
- Show the pictures to the children and talk about the blue color in each picture.
- Ask the children to look for blue in their clothes.
- Look for blue in the room.
- Encourage them to be observant by suggesting other places to look.

    Look at the ceiling

    Look at the wall

    Look at the pictures

- Ask them to name other blue things like foods, cartoon characters, etc.
- Play this game using other colors.

Finding Colors

Teaches Color Recognition

- Shine a flashlight on objects in the room..
- Tell the children that you are looking for something red.
- Ask them to say, "Hooray," when the flashlight finds something red.
- Repeat this game using different colors.
- Try the game with shapes.

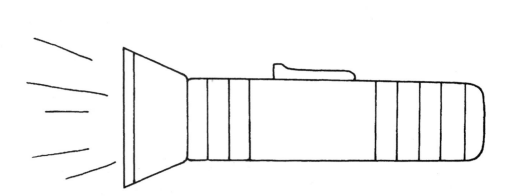

Color Games

Riddley, Riddley, Ree

- Start the game by saying:

  Riddley, riddley, ree,

  I see something you don't see,

  And the color is _____.

- The children get three tries to guess the object you see.
- Continue the game, asking one of the children to say the rhyme.
- Try the game substituting shapes, numbers, etc. for color.

Alike and Different

Improves Observation Skills

- Pick out a characteristic common to several children and ask all the children, one by one, to answer either "yes" or "no."
- For example, choose blue eyes.
- Ask each child, "Do you have blue eyes?"
- After all have answered, ask the blue-eyed children to stand and be applauded by the rest of the children.
- Say "Let's clap for all of the blue eyes."
- Repeat the game, but ask for brown eyes.
- After all the children have had a chance to stand and be applauded, point out that some eyes are alike and others are different.

Color Hopping

Teaches Color Recognition

- Tell the children that when you say "go," you want them to touch as many blue things in the room as they can find.
- They must hop to the blue things, however.
- Say "stop."
- Ask the children to name all the blue things they touched.
- Play this game using any color.
- Play this game with textures, by asking them to find and touch soft things, for example.

Color Games

Listening for Colors

Improves Listening Skills

- Ask the children to listen for colors in the songs that you are about to sing.
- Sing a song that mentions a color.
- Here are a few suggestions.

    "Yellow Bird Up High in the Banana Tree"

    "When the Red, Red, Robin Comes Bob, Bob, Bobbin' Along"

    "Oh, the Yellow Rose of Texas"

Breakfast Colors

Develops Memory Skills

- Ask the children what they ate for breakfast.
- Talk about each food and its color.
- Then ask the children if they ate something yellow for breakfast. Compare yellow breakfast foods like eggs, margarine, cereal, etc.
- Next ask if anyone ate something white for breakfast. Continue asking about other colors.
- Play this game naming lunch or dinner foods.
- This game really helps children think about what food looks like.

Color Games

Can You Name ____?

- Sing the following song to the tune of "London Bridge Is Falling Down."
- Leave out the final word for a child to fill in.
- If color is the subject, the song goes like this.

    Can you name your favorite color,

    Favorite color, favorite color?

    Can you name your favorite color?

    (Tell us, Brian)

    _____.

- Brian names his favorite color.
- Play this game using various subjects like trees, animals, flowers, food, etc.

Be a Color

- This game helps children associate colors with living objects. Give them ideas to act out that will help them to make these associations.

    Be a yellow, buzzing bumblebee

    Growl like a black bear

    Eat some red cherries

    Carve an orange pumpkin into a jack-o'-lantern

- Make up other color activities.

Color Words

- Identify things in the room that are red.
- Walk around the circle and say, "Tria, are you wearing red?"
- Tria will look at her clothes and tell you if she is wearing red.
- Encourage the children to answer in full sentences.
- Each day try a different color.

Counting Games

Family Talk

- Talking about families gives young children a chance to become familiar with different kinds of families.
- Recite the following rhyme.

  How many people live at your house?

  How many people live at your house?

  Can you count them? Can you count them?

  How many people live at your house?

- Ask a child to volunteer this information about his family.
- Encourage the other children to count together as the child names the people who live at his house.

Number Fun

Develops Number Recognition

- Write one number on a card or sheet of paper.
- Prepare one card for each number, up to ten.
- Pass out the cards to the children.
- Sing to the tune of "Are You Sleeping":

  Where is two? Where is two?
      (child with the number two holds it up in the air)

  There you are, there you are.

  We're so glad to see you,

  We're so glad to see you,

  Run away, run away.

- Continue with other numbers.
- With a group of young children, begin with the number one and proceed in numerical order.
- With a group of older children, sing the numbers in random order so that they do not know which number to expect next.

Counting Games

Teddy Bear Fun

Teaches Counting Skills

- Imagine that every child in the room could have a teddy bear.
- Make a chart with each child's name on it.
- Let the children count how many teddy bears they will need to make sure everyone has a bear.
- Add one more bear for each teachers.

Pocket Counting

Improves Counting Skills

- Ask the children to look at their clothes.
- Ask each child to count the number of pockets she has.
- Each child tells the rest of the children how many pockets she has.
- Decide which child has the most pockets.
- Which children have the same number of pockets?
- How many children have the same number of pockets?

Let's Count

Builds Counting Skills

- This is an excellent game to play when you have only a few minutes.
- Count anything.

    How many children are wearing blue?

    How many windows are there in the room?

    How many children have on white socks?

- Each time you ask a question, count out loud to find the answer.

Counting Games

Three Sit Down

- Ask the children to stand in a circle.
- Tell them to count off by threes.
- Every child that says the number three, sits down.
- With the children still standing, count off by threes again.
- Continue playing until every child is seated.
- This game provides good practice in counting.

Body Counting

- Count parts of the body with the children.
- Name a part of the body.
- When all the children have found that part of their own bodies, count them together.
- Let the children take turns naming parts of the body.
- Hands, fingers, knees, toes, ears and elbows are very popular.

Counting Games

Musical Math

- This game is a great counting exercise.
- Sing the popular song "If You're Happy and You Know It" and change the words to give counting directions.

    If you're happy and you know it, clap two times...

    If you're happy and you know it, hop two times...

    If you're happy and you know it, jump four times and snap two times...

- Give older children more complicated directions.

Three Times Around

- This game is a lot of fun.
- Form a circle.
- Hold hands, walk around in the circle and recite the following poem.

    Three times around went the gallant ship,

    And three times around went she.

    Three times around went the gallant ship,

    And we sank to the bottom of the sea.

- Fall down after saying, "sank to the bottom of the sea."
- Keep adding numbers and count as high as you want.

    Four times around...

    Five times around...

    Ten times around...

- Always end with "sank to the bottom of the sea."

Counting Games

Movement Counting

- Have the children stand up.
- Give directions for moving in different ways.

    Jump one time

    Hop two times

    Tiptoe three times

    Turn four times

    Gallop five times

- Continue with higher numbers but no higher than the children will understand.

Calendar Math

Teaches About Numbers

- Tape a blank piece of paper over one of the dates on the calendar.
- Ask the children to guess which number is covered.
- After they have guessed, lift up the paper to see if they were correct.
- With older children, try covering more than one number.

Four Seeds

Enhances Coordination

- Choose one child to be the mouse, one to be the crow, one to rot and one to grow.
- Point to each child as you say the poem.

    Four seeds in a hole.

    Four seeds in a hole.

    One for the mouse,

    One for the crow,

    One to rot,

    And one to grow.

- After reciting the poem, count the children by holding up four fingers one at a time.
- Repeat with different children.

One Potato

Teaches Fun With Friends

- This popular counting game has been a favorite of children for many years.
- Sit the children in a circle.
- Ask them to make fists with both hands and hold their fists in front of their bodies.
- Choose a leader to tap each fist as all the children say, "One potato, two potato, three potato, four. Five potato, six potato, seven potato, more."
- The fist that is tapped on the word "more" goes behind the child's back.
- Start the game again and continue until only one fist remains.
- That child becomes the leader for the next round of the game.

Counting Games

Scramble Five

- Start this game with a group of five children.
- Give each child a card with one number on it.
- Together the children have all the numbers one through five.
- Show the children how to line up in numerical order.
- Place the child with the number one card first.
- Ask for the child with the number two card to stand next to number one.
- Continue until the entire group is lined up in order.
- Call out "scramble."
- Tell the children to mix themselves up.
- Call out "unscramble."
- Let the children try to put themselves back in numerical order.

Count with Me

- This poem offers a playful way to teach counting.
- Hold up three fingers each time you say one, two, three.

    Count with me:

    One, two, three.

    Three little dogs rolling on logs.

    Count with me:

    One, two, three.

    Three little pigs wearing wigs.

    ...Three yellow ducks driving trucks.

    ...Three brown bears combing their hair.

Counting Games

The Zoo

Improves Counting Skills

- Try this fingerplay for a fun-filled counting time.

    One, one, the zoo is lots of fun. (hold up one finger)

    Two, two, see a kangaroo. (hold up two fingers)

    Three, three, see a chimpanzee. (hold up three fingers)

    Four, four, hear the lions roar. (hold up four fingers)

    Five, five, watch the seals dive. (hold up five fingers)

What's the Number?

Teaches Number Recognition

- Take a deck of playing cards.
- Show them one by one to the children.
- Identify the number on each card with the children.
- Show them the cards, numbers one through ten.
- Give each child one card.
- Ask the children to line up in correct numerical order.
- Take the cards back.
- Give another card to each child in random order.
- Let the children put themselves into correct numerical order.

Counting Games

Singing Subtraction

- Many songs and chants feature counting backwards.
- Children love to count backwards in "Five Little Monkeys."

  Five little monkeys jumping on the bed,

  One fell off and bumped his little head.

  Called for the doctor,

  And the doctor said,

  "No more monkeys jumping on the bed."

  Four little monkeys...

  One little monkey...

  And the doctor said,

  "Put those monkeys back to bed."

- Other songs and chants include:

  Five Little Ducks

  Ten in the Bed

  Five Little Pumpkins

Countdown

- Ask the children to count the number of times that a particular word appears in a song.
- Start with "Mary Had a Little Lamb."
- Ask the children to tell you how many times the word "lamb" is sung.

  Mary had a little lamb,

  Little lamb, little lamb.

  Mary had a little lamb,

  Its fleece was white as snow.

- If there is a difference of opinion, repeat the song.
- Other good songs are:

  The Wheels On the Bus ("wheels")

  London Bridge Is Falling Down ("down")

  Jack Be Nimble ("Jack")

Counting Games

Five Little Children

Develops Rhyming Skills

- Recite the following poem with the children and let them fill in the missing words.

    Five little children playing on the shore,
    One went away and then there were _____.

    Four little children sailing on the sea,
    One went away and then there were _____.

    Three little children mixing up a stew,
    One stopped stirring and then there were _____.

    Two little children playing in the sun,
    One went home and then there was _____.

    One little child playing all alone,
    Went to talk to friends on the telephone. (pretend to pick up a phone and talk)

Ten Fluffy Chickens

Improves Counting Skills

- Here is a nice fingerplay that is perfect when you have just a few minutes.

    Five eggs
        (hold up five fingers)
    And five eggs
        (hold up five more fingers)
    And that makes ten.
    Sitting on top is the mother hen.
        (pretend to be sitting on eggs)
    Cackle, cackle, cackle, cackle,
    What do I see?
    Ten fluffy chickens as yellow as can be.

Counting Games

Number Three

Teaches About Numbers

- Clap your hands and count out loud, "one, two, three."
- Ask the children to clap and count with you, "one, two, three."
- Ask the children to move different parts of their bodies three times and to count out loud each time that they move.

    Open and close your eyes three times

    Click your tongue three times

    Shake your head three times

    Hop three times

    Take three steps forward and then backwards

- Make up other body movements.
- Play this game using any number of movements.

Number Hopping

Develops Motor Skills

- Put a straight line of masking tape on the floor. The line should extend several feet.
- Make cards with one number on each card.
- Tape them sequentially to the straight line.
- Give directions to one child at a time. "Hop to number three. Jump to number seven," etc.
- When the children understand how to play the game, let them give the directions.

Counting Games

Three Little Fish

Practices Counting Skills

- Divide the children into groups of three.
- Recite the following poem and perform the actions.

  *Three little fish swimming in
  the water,*

  Swimming in the water,

  Swimming in the water.

  *Three little fish swimming in
  the water,*

  *Bubble, bubble, bubble,
  bubble,*

  Splash!!

  By Jackie Silberg

- On the word "splash" one child in
  each group falls to the ground.
- Repeat the rhyme saying "two little fish."

Five Currant Buns

Teaches Subtraction

- Choose five children to be the currant buns.
- Ask them to sit on the floor in a row.
- Choose five more children to take away the currant buns.
- Recite the poem.

  Five currant buns in a baker's shop,

  Big and round, with some sugar on the top.

  Along came (child's name) with a penny to pay.

  Who bought a currant bun and took it right away?

- One of the "takers" pretends to pay a penny.
- Then she takes the arm of one of the "currant buns" and goes to another part of
  the room.
- Repeat with "four currant buns."

Counting Games

Adding Rhymes

- Children enjoy both these adding rhymes.

  There were two little dogs sitting by the door,

  Two more joined them and then there were four.

  Four little dogs playing some tricks,

  Two more joined them and then there were six.

  Six little dogs barking at the gate,

  Two more joined them and then there were eight.

  One little bird sitting in the tree,

  "I'm as lonely as can be."

  Along came another one and stopped to rest,

  Now there were two birds in the nest.

  There were two little birds sitting in the tree,

  "We're as lonely as can be."

  Along came another one and stopped to rest,

  Now there were three birds in the nest.

- Continue adding numbers. With younger children, stop between three and five; with older children, go up to ten. Then say the last verse.

  All the little birds sitting in the tree,

  The branch began to sway.

  "Oh, oh, look out, we're going to fall,"

  So all the little birds flew away.

Silent Counting

- Sit the children in a circle on the floor.
- Clap four times and count out loud as you clap, "One, two, three, four."
- Ask the children to clap and count with you.
- Clap four times again, but this time count silently.
- Move your mouth so that the children can see you counting but cannot hear the words.
- Ask the children to imitate you as you count silently.

Counting Games

The Falling Leaves

Practices Subtraction

- Ask five children to come to the front of the room and pretend to be leaves flying in the air.
- Recite this poem.

    Five little leaves so bright and gay were dancing about on a tree one day.

    The wind came blowing through the town,

    Pheeew! (blow like the wind)

    One little leaf came tumbling down. (one child tumbles to the ground)

- Ask the class how many leaves are left.
- Repeat the game with "four little leaves."

Go to Bed

Develops Coordination

- Recite this poem with the children.
- Ask them to hold up one finger for first, two for second and three for third.

    Go to bed first,
        A golden purse.

    Go to bed second,
        A golden pheasant,

    Go to bed third,
        A golden bird.

Counting Games

Shaking Dice

- Show the children how to shake a pair of dice.
- Let each child shake the dice and count the number of dots facing upwards.
- After everyone has had a turn, play the game again. Ask each child to count the number of dots and hold up an equal number of fingers.

How Many Parts?

Practices Balance

- Ask the children if they can walk on two parts of their bodies (two feet, two knees, one foot and one hand, etc.).
- Ask the children if they can walk on three parts of their bodies (two legs and one arm, two knees and one elbow, etc.).
- Try walking on four parts of the body.
- Help the children explore all the different ways to walk on four parts.
- How about five parts?

Drama Games

Stop the Sound

Encourages Creative Thinking

- This is a great game for challenging children's imaginations.
- Tell the children that they are going to choose a sound to make. They can make that sound as long as the scarf is in the air.
- Once the scarf touches the ground, the sound must stop.
- Sounds can be anything from animal sounds to laughing, crying or humming.
- Say "ready, set, go" and toss the scarf into the air.
- Play the game to model starting and stopping a sound for the children.

Do You Feel?

Teaches About Feelings

- Talk with the children about different feelings.
- Ask them to look sad, then happy, angry and scared.
- Invite one child to come to the front of the class and make a face that shows one of these feelings.
- Ask the others to guess what kind of face he is making.
- A good follow-up activity to this game is to look through magazines and find pictures of people who are happy, sad, angry or scared.

Drama Games

Oh, Doctor Jane

- Divide the children into groups one and two.
- Let them suggest how to act out the dialogue.

    Group One: *Oh, Doctor Jane.*

    Group Two: *Oh, Doctor Jane.*

- Continue with Group One speaking a line, Group Two repeating it.

    I've got a pain. (repeat)

    My head is hot. (repeat)

    I don't want a shot. (repeat)

    Oh, Doctor Jane. (repeat)

    I've got a pain. (repeat)

    Please help me, Doctor, to get better. (both groups together)

    Open up wide. (repeat)

    Let's look inside. (repeat)

    Your throat is red. (repeat)

    Better go to bed. (repeat)

    And drink your milk. (repeat)

    And get some rest. (repeat)

    You will feel better in the morning. (both groups together)

    By Jackie Silberg

Red Light Stop

Practices Color Recognition

- Hold up a fairly large red card or sheet of paper.
- Explain that the red light on the street means you should stop.
- Hold up a green card and an orange card and explain what they mean.
- Line the children up.
- Tell them to start walking to the opposite side of the room.
- When you hold up the red card, they stop.
- When you hold up the green card, they walk.
- When you hold up the orange card, they wait.

Drama Games

Turtle

Encourages Imagination

- This popular poem is wonderful to act out.

> There was a little turtle
> That lived in a box. (put hands together to make a box)
> He swam in a puddle, (make swimming movements)
> And he climbed on the rocks.
> He snapped at a mosquito, (snap your fingers)
> He snapped at a flea, (snap your fingers)
> He snapped at a minnow, (snap your fingers)
> And he snapped at me. (snap your fingers)
> He caught the mosquito, (clap)
> He caught the flea, (clap)
> He caught the minnow, (clap)
> But he didn't catch me!! (make a proud face)

Keep a Straight Face

Teaches Fun

- This game requires partners.
- One child makes a face and keeps his expression fixed.
- It can be a silly face, a sad face, scary face, etc.
- His partner tries to make him laugh and lose his fixed expression.
- The only rule is no touching.

Drama Games

Unusual Walk

Enhances Imagination

- Take an unusual walk with the children.
- Start at one end of the room with everyone in a straight line.
- Walk at the front of the line.
- Ask the children to imitate your movements.
- Start walking and pretend to walk on different surfaces.

    Walk on a very hot sidewalk

    Walk in water

    Walk on ice cream

    Walk on rocks

    Walk on sand

- When you get to the other side of the room, ask the children if they can think of other ways to walk back.

If Your Body Could Talk

Teaches Body Awareness

- Pretend that different parts of your body can talk.
- Tell the children what each part of the body is saying, and ask them to act it out.

    Nose—I smell something yummy.

    Nose—I smell something yucky.

    Eyes—I'm happy.

    Eyes—I'm sad.

    Eyes—I don't understand.

    Shoulders—I don't know.

    Hands—Stop!

    Feet—I'm waiting.

    Elbows—Get away!

    Neck—I can't see you.

    Hands—I like you!

- With very young children, explain what these movements mean.

Gift Giving

Develops Creativity

- Ask one child to come forward.
- Tell this child that you are going to give him a gift.
- Without saying a word, put an imaginary ring on his finger.
- Ask the children if they know what the gift is.
- Talk with the children about different gifts that they would like to receive.
- Then ask if someone would like to give an imaginary gift to another person.
- If they are not sure how to, show them.
- This is a wonderfully creative game.

Family Photos

Promotes Imagination

- Talk about things that families like to do together.
- Choose one child to name the members of her family and talk about something that they did together. For example, her family went on a picnic.
- Pretend to take a picture of her family on a picnic.
- Invite different children to be in the picture, portraying members of her family.
- Let the child whose family you are photographing decide who will be in the picture and what they will do.
- For example, the mother is sitting on a blanket opening up a basket.
- The brother is next to the mother setting out the silverware for dinner.
- When all the characters are in the picture, take either a real or imaginary photograph of the group.
- You can play this game quickly every day with a different child's family.

Drama Games

Fun

Teaches Imagination

- Tell the children they are going to play follow-the-leader as they pretend to go to different places.
- Tell them where they are going and ask them to imitate what you do along the way.

    Go to the post office and mail a letter.

    Go to the supermarket and buy some groceries.

    Go to the zoo and look at the giraffes.

    Go outside to get on the school bus.

- You can play this game for as briefly or as long as you choose.

Face Passing

Develops Observation Skills

- Seat the children in a circle.
- Select a child to start the game.
- This child makes a face, then takes his face in his hands and pretends to pass it on to the next child.
- The next child makes the same face and passes it on to another child.
- Continue until all of the children have made the face and passed it on.
- Repeat the game with a new face.
- If the children have trouble deciding what face to make, suggest familiar animal sounds or expressions of emotion.

The Wizard

Enhances Imagination

- Choose a child to be the wizard.
- The wizard walks around the room.
- Everyone chants:

    I am the wizard, the wonderful wizard,

    Alakazaam, kazoo.

    I am the wizard, the wonderful wizard,

    And now I turn to YOU.

- At this point, the wizard taps someone on the head and says, "You are a ____."
- The wizard tells this child to be whatever he chooses, a cat, a monster, a fish, etc.
- This child then becomes the wizard.
- A three-pointed hat and a wand are wonderful props for this game.

Hello, Mr. Bus

Encourages Creativity

- Recite with the children:

    Hello, Mr. Bus,

    May I have a ride? (hold up thumb to hitch a ride)

    Oh yes, of course,

    Please step inside. (pretend to open up the bus doors)

    Put in some money, (drop money into the container)

    Step on the gas, (put foot on the gas)

    Vroom, vroom! (pretend to drive the bus)

    Not too fast!

Drama Games

Cross the Circle

Teaches Creativity

- Form a circle with the children.
- Have them count off by threes.
- Give them directions for crossing the circle.

  All the number ones cross the circle like a fish.

  All the number twos cross the circle like a fisherman.

  All the number threes cross the circle like a boat.
- Think of other related groups that could cross the circle.

  Circus: animals, ringmaster, tightrope walker

  Farm: animals, tractor, farmer

Finger People

Develops Coordination

- Enjoy doing this fingerplay with the children.

  Two fine gentlemen met in the lane. (hold thumbs up)

  Bowed most politely and bowed again. (bend thumbs toward each other)

  How do you do, how do you do,

  And how do you do again. (move thumbs as if they were talking to one another)
- Continue on with the fingerplay.

  Index finger—two fine ladies met in the lane...

  Middle finger—two nice teachers...

  Ring finger—two nice children...

  Little fingers—two little babies...
- With the "babies" it's fun to talk "baby talk."

May I Cross Your Bridge?

Promotes Cooperation

- This is a good game to play after the children know the story of "The Three Billy Goats Gruff."
- All the children line up on one side of the room.
- Choose one child to be the troll.
- The troll stands opposite the line of children.
- The children say, "Mr. Troll, Mr. Troll, may we cross your bridge?"
- Mr. Troll says, "You may hop across my bridge if you are wearing blue."
- All the children wearing blue hop across to the other side of the room.
- The rest of the children say, "Mr. Troll, Mr. Troll, may we cross your bridge?"
- Mr. Troll says, "You may jump across my bridge if you are wearing black."
- Each time the troll names a different color and movement.

Guessing Games

Cobbler, Cobbler

- Seat the children in a circle on the floor.
- Choose someone to be "it."
- That child stands in the middle of the circle holding a shoe.
- She gives the shoe to one of the others and says,

    "Cobbler, Cobbler, mend my shoe,

    Mend it well and I'll pay you."

- She hides her eyes.
- The children in the circle pass the shoe around behind their backs while saying,

    "Come find your shoe, it's now all done.

    See if you can find the one."

- When they finish chanting, the child who is "it" uncovers her eyes and points to the child whom she believes is hiding the shoe behind his back.

Favorite Toys

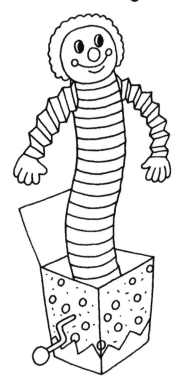

Teaches Imagination

- Talk with the children about their favorite toys.
- After they have named a few toys, ask them if they can pretend to be a certain toy.
- Start with something simple like a jack-in-the-box or a talking doll.
- Ask one of the children if she would like to pretend to be a toy in front of the group.
- See if the others can guess which toy she is.

Simple Charades

Develops Creative Thinking

- Pick one topic familiar to the children, for example, things to do in the water.
- As a group, act out different things that can be done in the water such as swimming, rowing, water skiing, splashing and fishing.
- Invite one of the children to come to the front of the group and act out a water activity.
- Encourage the others to guess what he is doing.

What's the Story?

Builds Thinking Skills

- Ask the children to identify a story by asking questions about it that can be answered with "yes" or "no."
- Think of a book or story that all the children love and begin by giving some kind of hint.
- For example, if the story is *Caps For Sale*, say that the story has lots of monkeys.
- Even if the children guess the book quickly, encourage them to ask questions anyway.
- Asking questions will help them recall the story and develop their language skills.

I Spy

Practices Observation Skills

- This popular game is fun for preschoolers.
- It's a wonderful game to fill an extra few minutes.
- One child is chosen to be "it."
- This child starts the game by saying, "I spy (someone who is wearing a green shirt with flowers on it)."
- The rest of the children try to guess who that someone is.
- Whoever guesses, becomes the next "it."
- Encourage the children to name inanimate objects as well. For example, "I spy something that is under the fish tank."

Guessing Games

Riddles

- Ask the children riddles about themselves.

    "I'm thinking of something on your face that is under your eyes."

    "I'm thinking of something that you put your shoes over."

- When the children become familiar with this game, make the riddles harder. For example, "I'm thinking of someone in the room who has a blue barrette in her hair."

- Encourage the children to make up their own riddles.

Good Morning, Teacher

- Choose one child to be the teacher.

- He sits at the front of the room with his back to the rest of the children.

- Choose another child to say, "Good morning, teacher" and encourage this child to disguise her voice.

- The teacher then replies, "Good morning, _____," naming the child who was speaking.

- If the teacher guesses correctly, he continues to be the teacher. If he does not, another child gets to be the teacher.

Guessing Games

Who's That Knocking?

- Choose one child to hide.
- She hides behind a door, a table or some other place from where she cannot see the rest of the children.
- Recite the following poem.

    Who's that knocking at my door,

    Who's that knocking at my door,

    Who's that knocking at my door?

    It's me, it's me at your door.

- Choose another child to say the words, "It's me, it's me at your door." Encourage that child to disguise his voice.
- The child who is hiding has to guess who is saying the "it's me" line.

I'm Thinking of...

Practices Observation Skills

- Say "I'm thinking of someone in this class who..."
- Add clues about this child.
- Describe his clothes, something that he is good at, any kind of positive observation.
- The rest of the children guess his identity.
- Children love to hear about themselves. This game also helps children get to know each other better.

Guess the Sound

Teaches Listening Skills

- Practice making sounds with your bodies.
- Have the children stamp their feet, snap their fingers and click their tongues.
- Ask one child to make a sound using some part of his body while the other children cover their eyes.
- The children try to guess what the sound is.
- Whoever guesses correctly, gets to make the next sound.

Guessing Games

What Is That?

Develops Concentration And Listening Skills

- The children try to identify sounds without seeing what is making the sound.
- Make a sound behind a door, easel or table.
- Tap your foot on the floor, crunch paper, clap your hands, ring a bell, make a kissing noise with your mouth, etc.
- Make one sound at a time, and see if the children can identify it.

Knock Knock

Teaches Listening Skills

- Ask the children to cover their eyes.
- Tap a pencil against an object several times.
- Ask the children if they know what the object is.
- Whoever guesses the answer, taps the pencil the next time.
- Places to tap the pencil include the floor, the door, a glass, a desk, a window and a drum.

Who Has the Roses?

Develops Listening Skills

- Choose one child to be the flower person.
- The flower person comes to the front of the room and turns her back so that she cannot see the rest of the children.
- The flower person says, "Who has the roses?"
- Choose one child to answer, "I have the roses."
- The flower person tries to guess who answered her question.

Mystery Sounds

Improves Memory Skills

- Prerecord three familiar sounds on a tape recorder, for example, a door slamming, water running and a radio playing.
- Say to the children, "I'm thinking of something that..." Describe one of the sounds.
- Play the tape and ask the children to tell you when they hear the sound that you described.

Identifying Sounds

Develops Thinking Skills

- Prerecord five sounds on a tape recorder, for example, a doorbell ringing, computer keyboard clicking, drumming, laughing or whispering.
- Play all of the sounds for the children. Play the first sound again and ask two questions: "Where would you hear this sound?" "Who would make this sound?"
- Continue playing each sound, one at a time, and ask the same two questions.
- After the children have talked about each sound, play all the sounds again. See if the children can remember the order in which they were played.

Guessing Games

Can You Guess the Sound?

- Choose three or four objects that make familiar sounds.

- Show the children each object and let them listen to the sound. Try to choose items that make different sounds.

- Ask one child to select an object while the others cannot see what she is choosing.

- The child hides behind a door or bookcase.

- She shakes the object, and the other children guess what object is making the sound.

- Play the game until each child has had a turn.

Rhythm Pictures

- Prepare several pictures of things that make rhythmic sounds or movements like a frog, a clock, an automobile, a piano, a washing machine and a top.

- Show the pictures to the children.

- Discuss with them the different rhythms suggested in each picture.

- Some things, like a car or a piano, perform at different rhythms. Talk about whether the rhythm is fast or slow, smooth or bumpy.

- Place the pictures face down.

- Choose one child to pick a picture and try to imitate the rhythm suggested by the picture on the card.

- The others try to guess which thing the child is imitating.

Imagination Games

Imagination

Teaches Creativity

- Lead all the children in pretending to be leaves high in a tree.
- A strong wind comes along and blows the leaves off the tree.
- Pretend to float very gently down to the ground.
- What do the leaves see as they float downward?
- Where do they land?
- Model the movement for the children.
- When they reach the ground, ask the children to talk about what they saw on the way down and where they landed.

Catching Butterflies

Develops Imagination

- The Chinese believe that if you set an animal free, it will bring you good luck.
- Children in Taiwan enjoy catching imaginary butterflies and then letting them go.
- Pretend you are catching a butterfly.
- Peek into your hand and describe your butterfly.
- What color is it? How big is it?

Imagination Games

Fortune-Teller

- One child is chosen to be the fortune-teller.
- A crystal ball (use any ball) and an interesting hat are props that make the game even more fun.
- The fortune-teller sits at a table.
- One child at a time comes forward and sits in the chair opposite him.
- All the children chant:

  Fortune-teller, fortune-teller,

  Can you see?

  When (child's name) grows up,

  What will (s)he be?

- The fortune-teller rubs the crystal ball and answers.
- If the fortune-teller needs help, offer suggestions. For example, "Damon loves to color. Maybe he will be a painter when he grows up." Or "Julia loves to build with blocks. Maybe she will be an architect or builder when she grows up."
- Talk with the children about different jobs and occupations.

What Would You Do?

- Talk with the children about different kinds of jobs. Talking about community helpers is often a good way to begin.
- Recite:

  What would you do,

  What would you do,

  What would you do if you

  Were a _____(name a job, for example, police officer)

- Choose one child at a time to reply.
- When that child is finished, ask the others if anyone else has ideas about what he would do if he were a police officer.

Can You Guess?

Develops Imagination

- Pretend to do different activities like hitting a baseball, jumping rope, putting on boots, etc.
- Make up many activities and do each of them with the children.
- Ask one child at a time to pretend to do something without telling the class what it is.
- When the child is finished, the others guess what he was doing.

A Different Simon

Develops Thinking Skills

- Play this version of Simon Says.
- In this game, Simon Says to make sounds rather than to do something.
- Simon says, "cough." Simon says, "sneeze." Simon says, "laugh." Etc.
- Instead of "Simon," let the leader use his own name or pretend to be his favorite character in a book.

Magic Wand

Teaches Imagination

- Make a magic wand, by rolling up a sheet of paper and taping it closed, or buy a commercial wand.
- Give the wand to a child and have her say:

  Abracadabra,

  Ziggety zee,

  You can be a _____.

- She points the wand to one child and tells him what to be.
- He acts out what he is told.
- Suggest to the child with the wand that it is often fun to tell someone to be an animal.

Imagination Games

Silly Singing

- Choose a song that the children already know, but change the words.
- For example, in "Yankee Doodle," instead of referring to "macaroni," say "pizza" or "ice cream," etc. Let the children make suggestions.
- One of the lines in "Skip to My Lou" is "Flies in the buttermilk, shoo, fly, shoo." Change flies to another insect and buttermilk to another drink. For example, "Ants in the orange juice, shoo, ants, shoo."
- Or try "Twinkle, twinkle, little bat."
- Ask the children to name other things that could twinkle, like snow, the moon, lightning bugs. Create new verses.

The Mailbox

- Read this poem to introduce a theme on mailing cards and letters.

    The mailbox on the corner

    Eats all the livelong day.

    It nibbles cards and letters

    In an amazing way.

    I wonder how it holds so
    *   much?*

    If I ate a pie or cake

    The way that box eats letters,

    I'd have a tummy ache.

- Talk about the mail carrier and how she delivers the mail.

Imagination Games

Making Wishes

- Talk about wishes with the children.
- Choose a child to be the fairy godfather or godmother.
- Give this child a magic wand.
- This child taps another child on the head with the wand to signal that it's time to make a wish.
- Recite:

    Make a wish,

    Make a wish,

    Now it's time to make a wish.

- The fairy godmother or godfather taps a child gently on the head, and that child makes a wish.

Naming Pictures

- Cut out interesting pictures from magazines and mount them on heavy paper.
- Show a picture to the children and title it. For example, a picture of children playing with a ball could be titled "Watch out, here comes the ball."
- Hold up the next picture.
- Let the children title the picture.
- If they don't have ideas, help them.
- After a few pictures, they will understand the game and enjoy using their imaginations.

Imagination Games

New Fairy Tales

- Think about ways to change stories familiar to the children.
- Talk to the children about your ideas.
- For example, change the "gruff" in "The Three Billy Goats Gruff" to "nice" or "kind." Encourage the children to suggest what a nice troll or a nice billy goat would say.
- Change Cinderella to a boy and give him a fairy godfather. Change the dialogue and events.
- These are wonderful experiments that develop creativity in children by showing them how to look at something familiar from a new point of view.
- Some other day, act out the new stories.

Rain Falling

- Divide the children into two groups.
- One group is the rain and the other is the sun.

    Rain: Rain falling

    Sun: Sun shining

    Rain: Rain falling

    Sun: Sun shining

    Rain: Rain falling, pitter patter

    Sun: Sun shining, burning, burning

- Keep adding descriptive words about the rain and the sun.
- Always start the sentence at the beginning so that the children will experience the sequence.
- Try having the sun group speak loudly and the rain group speak softly, or vice versa. Experiment with different voices.

Imagination Games

Wishing

Builds Language Skills

- Start the game by saying, "I wish I could take a trip to Disneyland."
- Ask every child to repeat the sentence, substituting places they would like to go for Disneyland.
- This is an excellent game to play when you only have a few free minutes. Other wishes include:

  I wish I could give a _____ to my mom.

  I wish I could buy a _____.

  I wish I could go to the zoo and bring home a _____.

Yummy

Develops Creativity

- Collect or draw pictures of food, for example, a banana, an apple, a glass of milk and a bowl of soup.
- Give one picture to each child.
- Have them stand in different parts of the room.
- Call out one of the foods: "banana."
- The children must run to the child holding the picture of the banana.
- Once they reach him, encourage them to pretend to eat a banana or to be a kind of animal that eats bananas.

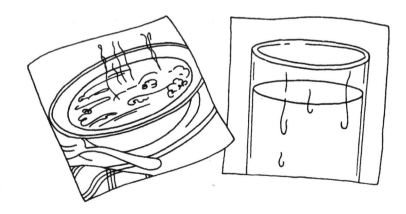

Imagination Games

Walking on Clouds

- Ask the children to pretend to walk on different surfaces.

  On clouds

  In deep mud

  On a tightrope

  On rocks

  On hot pavement

  Downhill

  Uphill

- Make up other ideas. Ask the children for their suggestions.

Boiling Hot

Teaches Creative Thinking

- This is a popular word game that gives children an opportunity to express their own ideas.
- Talk about the different things that they could put into the witch's pot to make a witch's brew.
- Get the children started with something gruesome like "spider legs," and they will understand the idea.
- Recite this rhyme to the children.

  Boiling hot, boiling hot,

  What will you put in the witch's pot?

- Choose a child to offer his suggestion.
- Show him how to incorporate his idea into the rhyme.

  Boiling hot, boiling hot,

  I'll put spider legs in the witch's pot.

- Finish by saying:

  Boiling hot, boiling hot,

  We are through with the witch's pot.

Imagination Games

Jelly in the Bowl

- Act out the following popular children's rhyme.

  Jelly in the bowl, (move like jelly in a bowl)

  Jelly in the bowl.

  Wibble, wobble, wibble, wobble,

  Jelly in the bowl.

- Help the children think of other foods to substitute for jelly.

  Cereal in the bowl. (move like cereal in a bowl)

  Cereal in the bowl.

  Crunchy, crunchy, crunchy, crunchy,

  Cereal in the bowl.

  Milk in the glass...slurpy, slurpy

  Pizza in the pan...chewy, chewy

Toss the Salad

Teaches Creative Thinking

- Choose one child to be the chef.
- Seat the others in a circle, and have the chef stand in the middle.
- Ask all the children in the circle to decide what kind of food they would like to be in a salad.
- Go around the circle and ask each child what food he is. Help children with suggestions, if needed.
- Then say "Chef, would you like some lettuce in your salad?"
- The chef answers, "Yes, I would like some lettuce in my salad."
- Whoever is the lettuce—and it can be more than one child—gets up, goes into the middle of the circle and stands next to the chef.
- Continue until every child is in the circle.
- Then say "Toss the salad!" All the children jump up and down.
- Say "Time to eat the salad." The children sit down again.
- Children really like this game!
- A chef's hat adds extra enjoyment.

Imagination Games

Pizza Pie

Improves Imagination

- With the children, invent actions to accompany the words.
- While saying the "yum yum" line, rub your stomach.

> *Give me a P,*
>
> *Give me an I,*
>
> *I've almost got my pizza pie!*
>
> *Two more Zs and one more A,*
>
> *We'll have a pizza pie today.*
>
> *Here's the sauce,*
>
> *Here's the cheese,*
>
> *Would you pass the pizza, please!*
>
> *Yum, yum, yum, yum.*

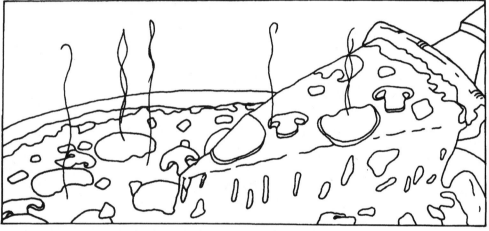

Fill in the Word

Teaches Imagination

- Begin a short story and let the children finish it. For example:

> *"Once upon a time there was a very beautiful princess who went walking in the woods. She thought she heard a voice singing a song. The singing got louder and louder. In front of her was a little house. When she looked inside, she saw a..."*

- Young children first playing this game often say a "mommy" or maybe a "queen."
- As they read and develop their imaginations, they will come up with other ideas to complete the story.

Imagination Games

Guess the Picture

- Cut large pictures of familiar objects from magazines or catalogs.
- Cover the pictures with strips of paper so that by removing the strips one by one, you will reveal the picture little by little.
- Ask the children to guess what the picture is.
- Remove one strip at a time, and they will begin to figure it out.

Ordering a Pizza

Develops Thinking Skills

- It is good for young children to practice organizing their thoughts.
- Ask the children if their parents have ever ordered a pizza by telephone.
- Talk about what information you give on the phone to place an order.

  What kind of pizza

  What size

  Your name

  Your address

  Your telephone

- Hold a conversation with a child in which you pretend to order a pizza.
- After playing this a few times with the children, you will see them begin to play this game with their friends.

Imagination Games

Nonsense Sentences

- Sing the song "Oh, Susannah" and explain to the children what is silly about the lyrics.

  It rained so hard the day I left,

  The weather it was dry.

  The sun so hot, I froze to death,

  Susannah, don't you cry.

- Invent nonsense sentences and ask the children to tell you what is funny about them.

  I put my bathing suit on to go ice skating.

  I ate my cereal from a glass.

  I washed my hands with sugar.

  I painted pictures with a hammer.

Language Games

Hometown Book

- Talk about places the children have visited around town.
- Encourage them to name these places, such as fast food restaurants, parks, the library or a parent's office.
- Send a note home to parents asking for photographs of places the children have visited.
- As the children bring in the pictures, mount them in a notebook.
- Whenever you have a few minutes, use the notebook to talk about places the children have visited.

May There Always Be

- This is a lovely Russian song translated into English.
- The words were written by a five year old child.

    May there always be sunshine.

    May there always be blue skies.

    May there always be mama.

    May there always be me.

- Talk with the children about what they wish there would always be lots of, forever.
- Substitute their answers for the words of the poem, for example:

    May there always be candy.

    May there always be daddies.

    May there always be kisses.

    May there always be me.

- Always end with "May there always be me."

Language Games

Photograph Fun

Develops Social Skills

- When you have a few extra minutes, talk with the children about photographs that you have taken during the year.
- Take photographs of the children doing various activities.
- Help the children remember the activities by looking at the pictures.
- Children love to see pictures of themselves.

Saying Hello

Builds Language Skills

- Each day say "hello" in a different language.
- Here are some suggestions.

    Ciao—Italian

    Bonjour—French

    Hola—Spanish

    Shalom—Hebrew

    Guten tag—German

    Allo—Russian

    Moshi—Japanese

Language Games

Changing Voices

Teaches About Sound

- What are ways voices can change?
- Changing the quality of the sound and the rhythm of the words is an excellent way to develop language skills.
- Pick a phrase like "I like ice cream" and say it several different ways.

  Hold your nose as you talk.

  Cup your hands around your mouth as you talk.

  Say the phrase loudly.

  Say the phrase softly.

  Pucker your lips as you talk.

  Put your hand over your mouth as you talk.
- Repeat by singing the words instead of saying them.

Acting Out Sounds

Encourages Imagination

- Let the children act out words—like thunder, fire engine or drums—that imply sounds.
- Make up a sentence using such words.
- Instead of saying the word, ask the children to make the sound and move accordingly, for example:

  First there were small raindrops and then there was loud
  _____. (thunder sounds)

  I see a fire. Here comes the _____. (fire engine sounds)

  The drummer played on the _____. (drum sounds)

Language Games

Awareness of Sounds

- Listening to sounds is like listening to words.
- Here are a few objects that make sounds that "speak."

    fire engine

    train whistle

    barking dog

    bells

    alarm clock

    telephone

    car horn

- Let the children imitate these sounds.
- One child can make the sound, and the others explain what the sound is saying.
- What kind of sound can you make to a friend? A whistle, a beep, a horn, a tap on a window?
- Can you tell someone something by just making a sound?
- How would you say "I like you" with a sound? (kiss)
- How would you say "I'm angry with you?" (stamp your feet)
- Try to find sounds in the environment that speak to you.

Happy Rhythms

- Seat the children in a circle.
- Give a rhythm stick to a child.
- The child holding the stick taps it on the floor and says, "My name is _____, and I like _____."
- She passes the stick to the next child.
- Children really enjoy this game.
- They discover that they like similar things.

Language Games

Let's Go Shopping

Develops Imagination

- Talk with the children about the different kinds of stores in which they like to shop.
- They will name toy stores, pet stores, supermarkets and bookstores.
- Decide together at which store you will pretend to shop.
- On the word "go," see how many things you can name and find in that store. Use a stopwatch.
- This game is a lot of fun. Playing several days in a row helps children to think of more words.

Sequencing Sounds

Teaches Sequencing Skills

- Ask the children to repeat the lines after you.

    I can cough, cough, cough. (make a coughing sound)

    (The children repeat the words and action.)

    I can (cough three times) and I can clap, clap, clap.

    (The children repeat the words and sounds.)

- Start at the beginning each time and add a new sound.
- It is a good idea to play the game the first time with three different sounds, and add more as the children become more experienced.
- Other sounds are:

    Sniffing with your nose

    Snapping your fingers

    Clicking your teeth

    Tapping your feet

Language Games

Classification Game

Teaches Associations

- Why not play a category game?
- Ask a question and see how many answers you can get.
- Try asking:

  What do you like on pizza?

  What are some things that fly?

  How many colors can you name?

Counting in Spanish

Improves Counting Skills

- Counting games are an easy way to introduce young children to a foreign language.
- Count in Spanish.

  uno

  dos

  tres

  quatro

  cinco

  seis

- Use the time while doing chores to practice a different language.
- If a child knows another language, this offers a great opportunity for her to share her language with other children.

Texture Talk

Teaches About Textures

- Ask the children to feel their clothing and to raise their hands if they feel something soft.
- Continue with this texture game by asking for clothes that feel silky, rough, cool, smooth, etc.
- If one child has a smooth shirt, let him compare its feel with another child's smooth clothing.

Language Games

Body Words

- Practicing speech patterns is a wonderful pre-reading experience.
- Children like to say new words.
- They will repeat the same word over and over because they enjoy saying it so much.
- Say the words "ice cream."

  Say it with your mouth.

  Say it with your hands. (clap hands to the syllables)

  Say it with your head. (move head up and down to the syllables)

  Say it with your feet. (stamp feet to the syllables)

  Say it with your eyes. (blink eyes to the syllables)

Days of the Week

- Name the days of the week by clapping your hands together while the children guess which day you are clapping.
- You will soon see that all the days have the same rhythm except Saturday.
- Clap your hands as you say, "Sun-day, Mon-day, Tues-day, Wednes-day, Thurs-day, Fri-day, Sa-tur-day."
- Clap the days of the week again, naming them in a soft voice until you come to Saturday, which you name in a loud voice.

～ ～ February ～ ～

Sunday	Monday	Tuesday	Wednesday	Thursday	Friday	Saturday
		1	2	3	4	5
6	7	8	9	10	11	12
13	14	15				

Language Games

Word Sharing

- Pick a word that the children know.
- If you have recently taken a field trip, try using a word that will remind them of the trip.
- For example, use the word "farm" and ask the children to suggest words related to it.
- Encourage them to name farm animals.
- As they talk about the animals they saw on the farm, expand their thinking by suggesting a different kind of farm word.
- For example, mention wheat and how it smells. Ask about sounds they might associate with a field of wheat.
- This game can be simple or complicated to play.

Vocabulary Fun

Develops Vocabulary

- This game builds vocabulary wonderfully.
- Pick an unfamiliar word and explain it to the children, for example, "pediatrician."
- After you have told the children what the word "pediatrician" means, ask questions that require a "yes" or "no" answer.

    Have you ever gone to a pediatrician?

    Does a pediatrician look at your eyes?

    Does a pediatrician make ice cream?

Language Games

Making Sentences

Teaches Sentence Structure

- Tell the children that you are going to say a sentence using the words "rabbit" and "carrot."

- Create a sentence using both words; for example, "The rabbit ate a carrot."

- Suggest two other words with a similar relationship, for example, "dog" and "bone."

- Ask the children to make up a sentence using those two words.

- As the children become more sophisticated in playing this game, increase the number of words.

Interesting Talk

Practices Language Skills

- Explain to the children that you would like them to finish a sentence.

- Begin by saying, "My favorite place to visit is the park because..."

- Ask them to think about why the park is a favorite place.

- Begin other sentences for the children to finish.

- Younger children may have difficulty with this game. Try stimulating and building their vocabulary in advance. Then try the game again.

Language Games

Looking at Pictures

Encourages Thinking Skills

- Show the children a picture containing at least two characters and some activity, for example, an adult helping a child put on boots.
- Discuss the picture with the children.
- Ask questions about the picture that require descriptive answers. For example, "What color is the child's hair?"
- Ask the children to tell you what happened before the child put his boots on, and what is going to happen after his boots are on.

Sequencing Fun

Enhances Sequencing Skills

- This is a simple variation of a traditional word game.
- Choose a topic that all the children will know—like toys!
- Start with the sentence, "I am going to the toy store to buy a teddy bear."
- The next child repeats the sentence, adding another toy.
- Keep going from child to child, always repeating and building upon the previous sentence.
- Children like this game.
- If they have trouble remembering the sequence of toys, another child will probably help them.

Introductions

Builds Social Skills

- Sit the children in a circle on the floor.
- Choose a child to start the introduction game.
- This child says her name, then introduces the child next to her. For example, "My name is Susan, and I would like to introduce Gregory."
- Gregory gives his name and introduces the child next to him. This is a good way to learn names as well as how to introduce others.

Language Games

I See My Nose

| Teaches Body Awareness |

- Talk about all the parts of the face and head.
- Name the parts and touch them.
- Eyebrows, eyelashes, nostrils, cheeks are parts that some children may not know.
- Sit the children in a circle.
- Pass a mirror around the circle.
- Ask each child to say, "I see a _____."
- They are to name and touch one part of their face.

Job Talk

| Develops Social Skills |

- Ask the children about the jobs that members of their families go to each day.
- Pick one family member, for example, the father.
- Ask questions such as:

    What kind of work does your father do?

    What work does your father do at your house?

    What does your father do for fun?

    What games does your father like to play?

- The next time choose another family member to talk about.
- NOTE: Be sensitive to the children's family situations.

Language Games

Language Rhythm

Teaches About Syllables

- Ask the children what they like about springtime.
- Choose three words from among their suggestions, for example, flowers, outside and birds.
- Clap the rhythm of the syllables in these three words with the children.
- Clap each word several times in a row.
- "Flowers" has two syllables, so it gets two claps. "Outside" also has two syllables. "Birds" has only one syllable.
- Chant with the children, clapping and repeating the three words over and over: flowers, outside, birds.
- As you say each syllable, be sure to clap on the beat.
- Choose words about other subjects.

Wind, Wind, Sugar Baby

Develops Coordination

- Chant the following:

    Wind, wind, sugar baby. (wind hands around each other)

    Wind, wind, sugar baby.

- Continue, substituting other motions.

    Pull, pull, sugar baby... (pull hands back as if to stop a horse)

    Hammer, hammer, sugar baby... (hammer fists together)

    Clap, clap, sugar baby... (clap)

    Point to the ceiling, sugar baby... (point to ceiling)

    Point to the floor, sugar baby... (point to floor)

    Point to the windows, sugar baby... (point to windows)

    Point to the door, sugar baby... (point to door)

    Clap your hands together, sugar baby... (clap)

    Clap one, two, three, sugar baby... (clap one, two, three)

- End with:

    Take your hands and place them on your knees.

Language Games

Little Lamb

Practices Language Skills

- Recite the poem, acting out each line.

    Little lamb says,
    "Baa, baa, baa."

    The flying crow says,
    "Caw, caw, caw."

    My, you're funny,
    Ha, ha, ha.

    Talk to the baby,
    Ma, ma, ma.

    Make a picture,
    Draw, draw, draw.

    Dance with me,
    Cha, cha, cha.

    Eat your dinner,
    Slaw, slaw, slaw.

Happy and Sad

Enhances Language Skills

- Talk with the children about what makes them happy and what makes them sad.
- Ask the children to make happy faces, then sad faces.
- Ask one child to stand in front of the others and make either a happy or sad face.
- Tell the others to guess which it is.
- Ask each child to tell if he is happy or sad and why.

Language Games

The Doorbell Game

- Sit the children in a circle and recite to them:

    Ding, dong, ding, dong,
    Who is ringing the doorbell?
    Ding, dong, ding, dong,
    Who do you think it is?

- Say "ding, dong" to sound like a doorbell.

- Ask the children who could be ringing the doorbell.

- Insert their answers into the poem one at a time.

    Ding, dong, ding, dong,
    Grandpa is ringing the doorbell.
    Ding, dong, ding, dong,
    I'm very glad you are here.

- Help the children think about who could be ringing their doorbell by suggesting friends, relatives and delivery people.

Catalog Fun

Develops Observation Skills

- Children love to look at toy catalogs.
- Let one child choose a toy in the catalog.
- Read the catalog description.
- Then ask the children how they would describe the toy.
- Help them by asking questions such as "What color is it?" "Is it large or small?" "Where can you play with it?"

Language Games

The Pizza Game

Encourages Creative Thinking

- This is a quick group activity that stimulates children's thinking and develops their language.
- Say a noun like "pizza" and ask the children for words that describe a pizza.
- Ask questions to help the children get started, if necessary. Questions like "What shape is it?" or "What does it have on top?" will help them describe a pizza.
- How many descriptive words can you come up with in a few minutes?
- Showing younger children a picture of a pizza will help them play this game.

Binoculars

Develops Language Skills

- This is a popular game and very effective in developing language skills.
- Each child picks a partner.
- The partners sit facing each other.
- One child in each pair makes imaginary binoculars with his hands. (Making circles with thumb and index fingers around his eyes.)
- Ask the child with the binoculars to describe his partner. Focus on a particular subject. For example, "What color are the clothes your partner is wearing?"
- Let the other child look through the imaginary binoculars.

Language Games

Pay Attention

- Choose four or five articles of clothing. Start with shoes, mittens, hats and belts.
- Discuss each item with the children as you place it into the basket.
- Cover the basket with a cloth or towel.
- Describe one of the items inside the basket.
- Ask the children if they remember what you are describing.
- Ask one child to come to the basket and pick out the article of clothing.

The Before Game

Teaches About Time

- The concept of time is so abstract that young children need a long time to understand it.
- Seat the children in a circle and say:

  (Keisha), can you tell me more

  Of what you did before—you woke up this morning.

- After Keisha answers, repeat the poem using another child's name.
- Ask this question about other times of the day.
- You can play this game often to help the children focus their thinking about time.

Language Games

What Goes With What?

Teaches Classification Skills

- Seat the children in a circle and hold up a spoon.
- Ask the children what goes with a spoon.
- Their answers might include a dish, a fork, food, etc.
- Talk about how all the answers are related to food.
- Hold up another object.
- See how many associations the children have with that object.

Storytelling Together

Builds Creative Thinking

- Place several objects inside a bag.
- Ask one child to pick out an object and say one sentence about it. Help him if needed.
- For example, if the object is a ball, suggest that he say, "Once upon a time, there was a ball."
- Ask another child a question about the ball. For example, "Where does the ball live?"
- After she answers, repeat the story they have created so far. "Once upon a time, there was a ball, and it lived in the toy box."
- Continue the story by adding new objects from the bag.

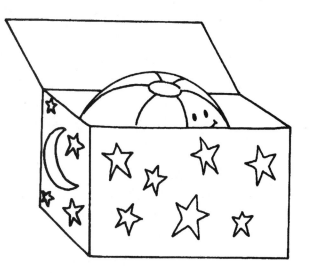

Language Games

Sequencing at the Supermarket

Teaches Sequencing Skills

- Talk with the children about what you do at the supermarket.
- Discuss the order in which you do things at the supermarket.
- First, you open the door.
- Next, you get a basket.
- Let the children decide what to put into the basket. There will be lots of discussion and probably some controversy.
- Once they have filled the basket, talk about standing in the check out line, filling the sacks and carrying them out to the car.
- This activity not only develops language skills, but helps children learn how to organize their thinking.

Family Language

Encourages Social Skills

- Discuss the names of family members: mother, father, brother, sister, grandmother, etc.
- Ask each child, "What do you call your mother?" There will be a variety of answers—mommy, mama, etc.
- Let each child share what he calls his mother.
- Continue asking the names of other family members.
- NOTE: Be sensitive to the children's family situations.

Saying Goodbye

Builds Vocabulary

- Talk about different ways to say goodbye. You can wave goodbye, shake hands goodbye and hug goodbye.
- Other words that mean goodbye include "See you later," "Have a good day" and "Bye-bye."
- Ask the children how they say goodbye to different people.
- How do they say goodbye to the mail carrier, the doctor, their mother?
- Don't forget "See you later, alligator" and "In a while, crocodile."

Language Games

Sentence Development

- Recite a short sentence to the children.
- Choose words they will understand, for example, "The car moves."
- Ask the children what color the car is.
- Repeat the sentence, including the color: "The red car moves."
- Continue asking questions and adding words to the sentence.
- Questions to ask include: "Where is the car going?" "Is the car big or little?"

Sounds Different

Teaches About Sound

- Talk about different kinds of sounds.
- Make the sounds as you discuss them.
- Sounds include:

    Scary sounds

    Loud sounds

    Soft sounds

    High sounds

    Low sounds

    Quiet sounds

    Squeaky sounds

- Name things that would make these sounds.

Language Games

Cheers

- Teach the children a few cheers.

    Hip, hip (hit hips twice)

    Hooray! (arms up in the air)

    Hip, hip (hit hips twice)

    Hooray! (arms up in the air)

    Our school's the best

    Every day! (wave arms back and forth in the air)

- Invent cheers about the children.

Categories

Promotes Language Skills

- Name a category, for example, food.
- Ask each child to name a type of food.
- Start with easy categories and gradually build up to more difficult ones like "Food we eat for breakfast."

Opposites

Teaches About Opposites

- These activities are playful ways to help children learn about opposites.
- Ask the children to:

    Sit down and stand up.

    Push and pull.

    Move their fingers fast through the air and slow through the air.

    Make a happy face and a sad face.

    Move their hands up and down.

    Shake their heads yes and no.

Language Games

Exploring Texture

- Help the children become aware of textures.
- Ask them to touch a variety of things in the room and help them describe what they feel.

  Is the floor cool, hard, smooth?

  Are your cheeks cold, warm, rough, smooth?

  Do your elbows feel different from your arms?

- This game offers an enriching pre-reading experience.

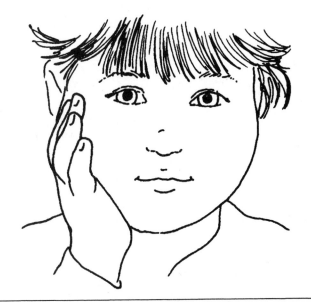

High and Low Game

Teaches About High And Low

- Ask the children to raise their hands high in the air.
- While their hands are in the air, encourage them to wiggle their fingers, wave their wrists and shake their arms.
- Ask them to put their arms down and make the same movements that they made with their hands high in the air.
- Ask the children to sit on the floor with one leg high in the air.
- Ask them to wave their ankles in the air, wiggle their toes and move their legs back and forth.
- Ask them to put their legs down and make the same movements that they made with their legs in the air.

Language Games

My Name Is

- Seat the children in a circle.

- Roll a ball to a child.

- Once the child catches the ball, he says, "My name is _____, and it starts with the letter ___."

- The child rolls the ball back to you.

- Roll the ball to another child and repeat the game.

- Always have the child roll the ball back to you. This will keep you in control of the game.

  Younger children will need help with this game.

Looking at Art

- Hold up a replica of a famous painting (by Monet or Picasso, for example) or any painting you enjoy.

- Talk about the picture with the children.

- How many different things do they notice about the picture?

  Colors
  Are they bright?
  How do they make you feel?

  Lines
  Are they straight?
  Are there short lines, long lines or both?

  Shapes
  Are there squares, triangles or circles?

  Textures
  Are there smooth or hard textures?

Language Games

Mr. Monday

Teaches The Days Of The Week

- Play this game with rhythm sticks or clapping.
- The children sit in a circle.
- Start the game by saying:

    Hey, Mr. Monday, play a song for me.

    Hey, Mr. Monday, play a song for me. (clap in a rhythmic pattern)

- Start with a simple rhythm, like clapping twice. The children repeat the pattern.
- Then say:

    Hey, Mr. Tuesday, play a song for me.

    Hey, Mr. Tuesday, play a song for me.

- Clap the same pattern or try a new one. The children repeat the pattern.
- Continue with each day of the week.
- Once the children know this game, they will invent their own clapping patterns.

Pointing

Develops Listening Skills

- Recite this poem and perform the actions with the children.

    Point to the window,

    Point to the door.

    Up to the ceiling,

    Down to the floor.

    Point to a table,

    Point to a chair.

    Point to a friend of yours,

    Sitting over there.

    Point to your head now,

    Point to your knee.

    Point to your elbow,

    Point to me!

- This poem offers nonverbal children an opportunity to communicate.

Language Games

If You Were a Farmer

Teaches About Occupations

- Have the children carry out these actions while singing this song to the tune of "Did You Ever See a Lassie?"

    Oh, if you were a farmer, a farmer, a farmer,

    Oh, if you were a farmer,

    What would you do?

    I would gather eggs for breakfast,

    For breakfast, for breakfast.

    I would gather eggs for breakfast,

    That's what I'd do. (pretend to put eggs into a basket)

    I would ride a horse to pasture... (pretend to ride a horse)

    I would milk the cows each morning... (pretend to milk a cow)

    I would feed the baby chickens... (throw seeds on the ground from a pail)

    I'd go plowing in a tractor... (steer a tractor)

Gibberish

Promotes Creativity

- Gibberish is a nonsense language. It consists of a lot of meaningless sounds, so any meaning has to be expressed through body language.
- Ask the children a question in gibberish and see whether they can, first, figure out the question, and then, answer by speaking in gibberish while shaking their heads either yes or no.
- Ask the children to talk to each other in gibberish.
- Young children love to play this game because they can create any sounds they want while talking in gibberish.

Language Games

Pack Your Bags

- Sit in a circle, clapping your hands to the following rhyme.
- Alternate clapping your hands on your knees with clapping your hands together.
- After the words "I will take," sustain the rhythm by clapping as one child names what he will take on the trip.

> *Pack your bags.*
>
> *We're going away.*
>
> *We're going to leave*
>
> *The first of May.*
>
> *Make a list of what you'll take.*
>
> *I will take _____. (child names something to take)*
>
> *By Jackie Silberg*

- Repeat the poem for the next child.

An Interesting Story

- Begin a story: "I was walking in the park one day, and what do you think I saw?"
- One child answers, "A house."
- All the children say, "What was in the house?"
- Another child answers, "A kitchen."
- All the children say, "What was in the kitchen?"
- The next child says, "A refrigerator."
- All the children say, "What was in the refrigerator?"
- The next child says, "A box."
- All the children say, "What was in the box?"
- The next child says, "Apples."
- Everyone says, "Yum, yum!"
- Once the children learn this story, they will love to tell it over and over.
- Invent other short stories with a similar sequencing pattern, for example, using country, farm, barn, kennel, dog, "Woof, woof!"

Language Games

Who Is It?

- Describe someone in the room by the clothes she is wearing.
- As soon as the child recognizes herself in the description, she jumps up and says, "I'm the one."
- Play another version of this game by describing objects in the room and seeing whether the children can identify the objects.

Going to Montreal

Teaches Sequencing Skills

- Young children really enjoy this game. Make the story longer or shorter.
- Sit in a circle. One child starts the game by saying:

    Oh, the country farmer went to Montreal.

    Oh, the country farmer went to Montreal.

- The next child says:

    Oh, the wife of the country farmer went to Montreal.

    Oh, the wife of the country farmer went to Montreal.

- The next child says:

    Oh, the child of the wife of the country farmer went to Montreal.

    Oh, the child of the wife of the country farmer went to Montreal.

- Continue the story, giving each child a new word to add to the sentence.

    Oh, the dog of the child of the wife of the country farmer went to Montreal.

    Oh, the tail of the dog of the child of the wife of the country farmer went to Montreal.

Language Games

The Shopping Song

- The object of this game is to name three words that begin with the same sound.
- The first time you play the game, give the words to the children in advance.
- As they learn more sounds, they will think of words on their own.
- This song is sung to the tune of "The Farmer in the Dell."

    We went shopping in the town,

    We went shopping in the town,

    In the window of a shop we saw... (name three things that start with the same letter)

- Suggestions include:

    book, ball, button

    pepper, popcorn, pig

    carrot, candle, cough drop

If You're Happy

- Sing "If You're Happy and You Know It."
- Then try the song with new lyrics.

    If you're happy and you know it...

    Point to someone wearing blue...

    Jump around in a circle...

    Throw a kiss...

    Stick out your tongue...

    Count to three...

Listening Games

Shhh, a Soft Sound

- Think about what is quiet and makes no sound.
- Show pictures of a fish swimming in the water, a butterfly, ice cream melting.
- Let the children act out the pictures.
- Ask them to name other things that do not make a sound.

A Participation Story

Enhances Listening Skills

- Tell this story to the children.
- Every time you say a word that implies a sound, make the sound. These words are:

  Walking (walk)
  Blowing (blow)
  Whistling (whistle)
  Loud (stamp feet)
  Jumped (jump)
  Heart (pound chest)
  Run (run in place)
  Kiss (throw a kiss)

- Tell the children to copy the sounds and movements you make.

    Once upon a time, there were two little children WALKING to school. The wind was BLOWING very hard, and the children started to WALK faster. The wind was BLOWING all of the leaves in the air and WHISTLING through the trees.

    All of a sudden there was a LOUD noise, and the two children JUMPED and grabbed each other. Their HEARTS began to beat faster, and they started to RUN. Finally, they reached the school, hurried inside the door and gave the teacher a big KISS.

- Invent your own story and choose your own words.

Sharing Game

Develops Language Skills

- Sit the children in a circle.
- Give one child a ball.
- Explain to the children that whoever is holding the ball will get to tell something about herself.
- For example, ask the child holding the ball what her favorite food is.
- When she finishes talking about her favorite food, she passes the ball to the next child.
- The only rule is that no one can talk except the child holding the ball.

Listening Games

Talking to My Friends

Builds Language Skills

- In order to play this game, either use two play telephones or use imaginary telephones.
- Pick up one of the phones and dial a child's phone number.
- As you dial, say the numbers out loud so that all the children can hear you.
- The child whom you called answers the second phone.
- After a short conversation, say "goodbye" and dial another child's number.

Sound or Silence

Improves Listening Skills

- This game is an enjoyable way to illustrate the difference between sound and silence, an important concept. In music, for example, the rests (silence) are just as important as the notes (sound).
- Ask the children to tiptoe around the room while you play music and to freeze in place when the music stops. Demonstrate what freezing means, if need be.
- Playing the music softly will help the children listen more carefully.

Loud Sounds

Teaches About Sounds

- This game is the opposite of the previous game.
- Think about what makes a loud sound.
- Show pictures of firecrackers, a motorcycle, drums.
- After the children have acted out the sounds, let them add more sounds to the list.

Circle Directions

Teaches How To Follow Directions

- Make a circle with masking tape on the floor.
- Ask the children to:

    Go in and out of the circle

    Walk around the inside of the circle

    Walk around the outside of the circle

    Crawl inside the circle

    Crawl in and out of the circle

    Put one foot in the circle and one foot out of the circle.

- Play the game with other shapes.

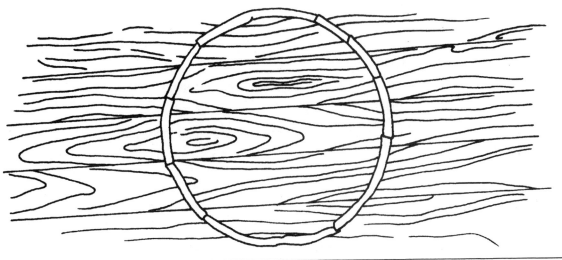

Chair Commands

Builds Listening Skills

- Sit the children in a circle.
- Explain to them that you are going to give them directions.
- Set a chair in the middle of the circle.
- Give several children specific directions. For example, "Everyone wearing the color red, come to the center of the circle and walk around the chair."
- You can also identify children by describing in detail what they are wearing. For example, "Someone wearing a blue dress, white socks and brown shoes, come to the circle and walk around the chair."
- Make this game simple or complicated according to the abilities of the children.

Listening Games

Who Do You Hear?

Develops Listening Skills

- Pre-record the children on a tape recorder.
- Tell them that each of them will say the same sentence into the microphone, and that later you will play a game to see whether they can recognize their voices.
- Ask them to say the same sentence, one at a time, into the microphone. Pick a positive statement like "This is a wonderful day," or "I love my school."
- The game begins after the recording is completed.
- Children love listening to the recording and trying to recognize each other's voices.
- This is a great game for developing listening skills.

Listen, Listen, Listen

Teaches Coordination

- This action poem requires careful listening.
- The children should stand in a circle with joined hands.

> *Step one and two. (take two steps to the left)*
>
> *Jump three and four. (take two little jumps and drop hands)*
>
> *Turn around quickly, (turn around)*
>
> *And sit on the floor. (sit on the floor with legs crossed)*
>
> *Clap one and two. (clap on "one" and "two")*
>
> *Shake your head three and four. (shake head on "three" and "four")*
>
> *Jump up again, (jump to a standing position)*
>
> *And be ready for more. (join hands again and start over)*

Listening Games

Moo, Cow, Moo

Improves Listening Skills

- Seat the children in a circle with one child designated to sit in the middle blindfolded.
- Everyone sings a favorite song like "Twinkle, Twinkle, Little Star."
- The child in the middle can stop the song anytime by saying, "Stop."
- When she says "Stop," the teacher taps another child on the head, who then says, "Moo, cow, moo."
- The blindfolded child tries to guess who is making the sounds.
- Try "bark, dog, bark" or "roar, lion, roar," etc.

Puppets

Develops Social Skills

- Ask the children to find a partner.
- The partners face each other.
- One child is a puppet and will do whatever the puppet master asks him to.
- Sing to the tune of "London Bridge Is Falling Down."

    (Puppet master) Puppet, can you stamp your feet, stamp your feet, stamp your feet?

    Puppet, can you stamp your feet,

    Stamp your feet?

    (Puppet) Yes, oh, yes, I'll stamp my feet, stamp my feet, stamp my feet.

    Yes, oh, yes, I'll stamp my feet,

    Stamp my feet.

- Repeat, substituting the following actions for "stamp my feet."

    Clap your hands

    Tickle your nose

    Scratch your back

    Wave your arms

    Jump up and down

- Change partners to give the other child a turn to be the puppet.

Listening Games

Thumbs Up, Please

Builds Listening Skills

- Ask the children to listen to the questions.

- Explain that their thumbs, not their voices, will answer the questions.

- If the answer to the question is "yes," they should put their thumbs up.

- If the answer to the question is "no," they should put their thumbs down.

- Questions to which yes is the answer could include "Do you like ice cream?" or "Do you like to play outside?"

- Those to which no is the answer could include silly questions like "Does a cow give juice?" or "Did you fly your airplane to school today?"

Surprise Animals

Teaches Sound Discrimination

- Choose two children to come up to the front of the room.

- Ask them to turn around so that they cannot see the faces of the other children.

- Ask the two children to think of an animal sound, but not to tell anyone what their sound is.

- At the signal, the children begin making their animal sounds and continue until you signal them to stop.

- The other children listen and identify the sounds they hear.

- When a sound is identified, the child making that sound sits down.

- After playing this game several times with two children, increase to three and eventually four.

- Sometimes the children will make the same sounds, and that's okay, because you want them to choose their own sounds.

- This is a marvelous listening game.

A Listening Game

Improves Concentration Skills

- Put three objects on a table, for example, a block, a book and a ball.
- Select three children to come to the table and pick up one object.
- Ask "Where is the block?" The child with the block answers, "Here is the block."
- Ask "Where is the book?" The child with the book answers, "Here is the book."
- Ask "Where is the ball?" The child with the ball answers, "Here is the ball."
- Practice this sequence a few times, then begin the game.
- Ask the questions in different tones of voice. Try asking in a loud voice, soft voice, sweet voice, whisper, gruff voice, nasal voice.
- Children will enjoy this game and think of other ways to change their voices.

Follow the Beat

Practices Listening Skills

- Clap your hands to different beats, some slow and others faster.
- Ask the children to clap their hands along with the beat.
- Make up stories to go with various speeds.
- Pretend to be different animals and change the kind of animal as the beat changes.
- A very slow beat could be an elephant, a medium beat goes with a kangaroo and a fast speed is fun for a squirrel.

Listening Games

Listen for the Word

- Pick three words about the same subject, for example, Halloween. The three words could be witch, cat and pumpkin.
- Sit in front of the children.
- Invent a story using these three words.
- Ask the children to listen for the words and, whenever they hear one, jump up.
- This becomes a lot of fun, especially if you use the words frequently in your story.

Mouth Sounds

Teaches Awareness Of Sound

- Making different sounds with your mouth is great fun and gives children a chance to become aware of the parts of the mouth.
- Suggested sounds include:

    Click your tongue

    Swallow

    Move your index finger across your lips

    Do the "raspberry"

    Blow inward and outward

    Smack your lips

    Cough

    Sneeze

- Can you think of others?

A Piano Game

Teaches About The Piano

- The word "piano" comes from the Italian word "pianoforte," which means soft and loud, because the piano can make both loud and soft sounds.
- Let the children watch as you play notes at the top of the piano keyboard. Talk about the "high" sound.
- Now play notes at the bottom of the keyboard and talk about the "low" sound.
- Ask the children to close their eyes and tell you whether you are playing a "high" sound or a "low" sound.

Another Piano Game

Teaches About The Piano

- Here is a nice fingerplay about the piano.

    Here is the hammer. (make a fist with one hand)

    Here are the strings. (spread the fingers of the other hand)

    Hit them together. (hit the hammer hand to the string hand)

    The piano sings. (sing "la, la, la")

    By Jackie Silberg

- Look at the inside of a piano and show the children the strings.
- Let them observe how the hammer on the key hits the string whenever you play a note.

Math Games

Can You Guess?

Teaches Estimating Skills

- This is an excellent game for developing the essential math skill of estimating.
- List the children's names on a large sheet of posterboard or paper.
- Laminate the posterboard and write on it with a transparency pen, allowing you to erase and change answers.
- Set out a jar of candy, a bowl of peanuts, a basket of rocks, a plate of grapes, etc.
- Ask the children:

  How many pieces of candy in the jar?

  How many peanuts in the bowl?

  How many rocks in the basket?

  How many grapes on the plate?

- As each child makes her estimate, either you or the child can write the estimate next to her name on the laminated board.

Matching Game

Teaches Matching Skills

- Have the children take off their shoes and place them in a pile.
- Mix them up to separate the pairs.
- Give a shoe to one child and ask her to find the matching one.
- After she has found it, she gives the pair to the owner.
- This game becomes easier as it continues, when there are fewer shoes to sort through, so choose the children who might find this task difficult later on in the game.
- Match other things besides shoes.

Math Games

Hand Dancing

Develops Sequencing Skills

- For each number, make a different hand motion.
- Start by saying "one" and clapping, waving or shaking your hand, etc.
- Say "two" and make a different motion with your hand.
- Start over, saying "one" and making the corresponding hand motion, then repeating "two" and that hand motion.
- Depending upon the age of the children, stop at two or count higher.
- A variation of this game is to count slowly, then faster and faster.
- This game provides excellent practice for counting as well as for sequencing.

Matching Stickers

Builds Friendship Skills

- Collect pairs of stickers.
- Put one sticker on each child's wrist.
- The children have to find their matching sticker.
- These children will be partners for the day, while waiting in line, helping each other get dressed, etc.

Guess the Category

Develops Sorting Skills

- This sorting game requires little time to play
- It is best played in a large open area where the children can move around.
- Sort the children by one criteria, for example, by colors.
- The children have to figure out what the criteria is.
- Tell a child wearing red to go to a certain part of the room.
- Tell a child wearing blue to go to a different part of the room.
- After all the children are sorted, ask them to try to figure out the criteria by which they were separated.

Math Games

Bead Patterns

Teaches Sequencing Skills

- Use beads of two different colors to create a pattern.
- Let the children watch as you assemble the pattern on the floor.
- For example, begin with a red bead, then a blue bead, a red bead, a blue bead, repeating the same pattern.
- After the pattern is established, ask the children what comes next.
- Once they have understood the concept of a pattern, change the bead pattern to two red, two blue, etc.
- Then try two red, one blue, etc.
- Make the patterns increasingly difficult, but be sure the children have understood a pattern before moving on.

Air Shapes

Teaches Cognitive Skills

- Sit the children in a circle.
- Draw a circle in the air with your index finger.
- Ask them to identify the shape.
- Continue the game, drawing a square, then a triangle.
- Ask the children to draw a circle, square, triangle.
- For younger children, this game may be too abstract. Show them a picture of the shape first, then draw it in the air.

Tall and Short

Develops Observation Skills

- Take a "tall" and a "short" walk around the room.
- Ask the children to observe what things are taller and what things are shorter than they are.
- Sit down and let each child describe something that they think is taller or shorter than they are.
- Ask each child to walk to the object.
- Ask the others if they agree.

Pencils!

Teaches Measuring Skills

- Give each child a pencil, preferably unsharpened.
- Show the children how to use their pencils to measure.
- Walk around the room and suggest things to measure.
- Ask the children if the objects are smaller, larger or the same size as the pencils.
- Encourage the children to use the pencils to measure parts of their bodies.
- Use blocks, toy cars or other objects as measuring tools.

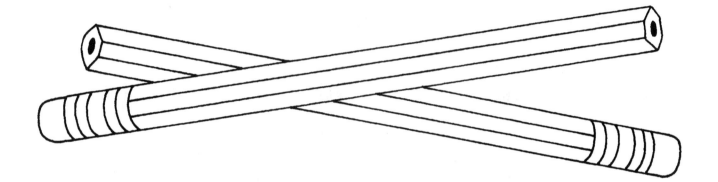

Musical Time

Teaches About Time

- Talk about length of time with the children.
- Ask them if they think one minute is a very long time.
- Set a timer for one minute. It is always amazing how long a minute can seem.
- Let the children pick a song that they enjoy.
- Set the timer for several minutes and sing the song over and over until the timer buzzes.

Math Games

Draw a Circle

Teaches About Shapes

- Recite the poem and perform the actions.

  Draw a circle in the air, (draw a circle in the air)
  Round as it can be.
  Draw a circle in the air,
  Draw it just for me.

  Draw a square in the air, (draw a square in the air)
  One, two, three, four. (count the corners)
  Draw a square in the air,
  One, two, three, four.

  Draw a triangle in the air, (draw a triangle in the air)
  One, two, three. (count the corners)
  Draw a triangle in the air,
  Just for me.

- Older children will enjoy this game, but it may be too abstract for younger children.

Looking at Leaves

Develops Sorting Skills

- Gather a few leaves and place them in a basket.
- Show each leaf to the children.
- Ask them if the leaf is pointed or round.
- Sort the leaves into two piles, pointed and round.
- This is a good sorting game for young children.

Math Games

Shape Throw

| Improves Shape Recognition |

- Cut out shapes and hang each on a ribbon.
- Give each child one shape to hang around her neck.
- Be sure the children can identify the shapes they are wearing.
- Direct the children to tap another on the back, calling on them by naming the shapes they are wearing. For example, "Triangle tap the circle" or "Square tap the triangle."

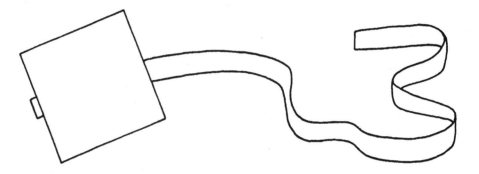

Triangle Dancing

Teaches About Triangles

- Divide the children into groups of three.
- Arrange the threesomes in the shape of a triangle.
- Make masking tape triangles on the floor, if need be.
- Face all the children toward the middle of their triangle so that they can see each other.
- Choose one child in each triangle to start the movements.
- Play instrumental music as the signal for that child to begin moving in place to the music.
- The other two children in each triangle copy the leader.
- When the music stops, the leader's turn ends.
- When the music begins again, the second child in the triangle gets to be the leader.
- Continue until the third child in each triangle has had a turn as leader.

Math Games

Shape Person

Develops Shape Recognition

- Cut circles, squares and triangles out of sponges.
- Choose a child to be the "shape person."
- The "shape person" chooses one shape, then sits in the middle of the circle of children with her eyes closed.
- Play instrumental music.
- When the music starts, the children pass the shape, chosen by the shape person, from child to child.
- When the music stops, whoever has the shape hides it behind his back.
- The "shape person" has to guess who has the shape.
- When she guesses correctly, the two children change places, and the game begins again.

Apple Math

Teaches Fractions

- Cut an apple in half.
- Show the children each half, referring to them as halves.
- Place the two halves together to make a whole apple.
- Take the two halves apart.
- Let each child put the halves together.
- It is important for the children to have hands-on experience in order to absorb the concept.

Match the Pan

Teaches About Matching Shapes

- Set a variety of pans and lids out on a table.
- Include rectangles, circles, squares and ovals, if possible.
- The children match each lid to its pan.
- This helps children understand that a square top does not fit on a round pan.
- It also helps them learn different shapes.

Math Games

Which Is First?

Builds Sequencing Skills

- This game helps children understand the concept of sequence.
- Bring two children to the front of the group.
- Put one child behind the other.
- Tell the children that the child in front is first, and the child behind is second.
- Ask the children, "Who is first, and who is second?"
- Another game is to make two sounds, one louder than the other.
- Ask the children, "Which sound is louder, the first or the second?"
- As the children begin to understand these concepts, add the word "third" to the game.

Where's the Peanut?

Teaches About Order

- Number five large paper cups one through five.
- Place the cups upside down in numerical order on a table or floor.
- Ask the children to close their eyes while you hide a peanut under one of the cups.
- Let one child at a time guess where the peanut is by asking, "Is it under the first cup?" "Is it under the second cup?" And so on through the fifth cup.
- Once the peanut is found, repeat the game with another child.

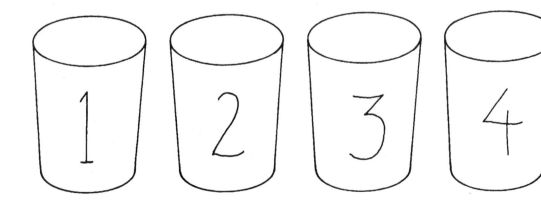

Math Games

Round and Straight

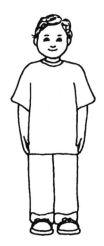

- Ask the children to make their arms straight, their hands straight, their entire body straight.
- Stand up straight.
- Lie down straight.
- Next, experiment with round, repeating all the movements, but making them round instead of straight.

Marble Fun

Teaches About More And Less

- Get two baskets.
- Put one marble in one basket and five marbles in the second basket.
- Ask the children to look into the baskets and decide which one contains more marbles.
- Rearrange the marbles, placing two in one basket and five in the other.
- Ask the children again which basket has more marbles.
- Keep playing the game, increasing the number of marbles in the first basket, making it harder each time.
- When the children are no longer sure which basket contains more, count the marbles.
- Play the game a different way, asking the children which basket has fewer marbles.

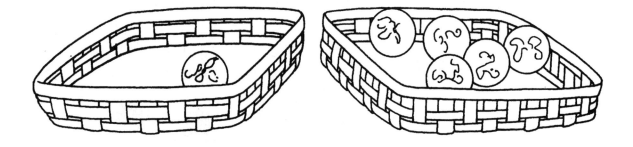

Measuring Spices

Teaches About Measurement

- Introduce children to the smell of spices. Start with cinnamon, cloves and nutmeg.
- Put a small amount of each spice into small glass bowls.
- Let the children smell each spice.
- Discuss how the different spices are used.
- Show the children a set of measuring spoons of different sizes.
- Select one spice and measure one tablespoon, one teaspoon, one-half teaspoon and one-quarter teaspoon onto a piece of wax paper.
- The children will see clearly the range from the larger to smaller amounts.

Measuring

Teaches About Measurement

- Show the children how to measure width and length with their arms. For example, measure a chair by placing your arm across it, saying, "This chair is one arm's length."
- Let the children measure various objects in the room with their arms.
- Walk across the room and count your steps as you do.
- Tell the children that it takes you ten steps to cross the room.
- Ask them to walk across the room and tell you how many steps it takes.
- The children may have different answers: all the answers are correct.
- Suggest other ways to measure distance and length with their bodies.

A Dotty Game

Teaches About Measurement

- Find a fairly long, flat surface, like the top of a table or a section of a wall.
- Place colored dots in a straight line along that surface.
- Show the children a basket full of pencils, sticks and other straight objects.
- Ask each child to choose something from the basket and measure it against the row of dots.
- Ask each child to figure out "how many dots long" that object is.

Math Games

Hop to the Square

Teaches About Shapes

- Cut out several squares, circles and triangles in various colors.
- Lay them on the floor.
- Call upon one child at a time.
- Give her a specific direction. For example, tell her to hop to the red circle, jump to the yellow square, etc.
- Continue until each child has had a turn.

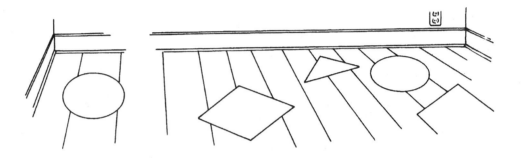

I Can Draw a Circle

Teaches About Circles

- Recite the following poem together.

    I can draw a circle,

    I can draw it in the air. (draw circles in the air)

    Round and round,

    I can draw it everywhere.

    I can draw a circle,

    I can draw it on the floor. (draw imaginary circles on the floor)

    Round and round,

    I can draw more and more.

    I can draw a circle,

    *I can draw it on your back. (children draw imaginary circles on
        each other's backs)*

    Round and round,

    I'll make you giggle if you wiggle! (children tickle each other)

Patterning with Shapes

Develops Sequencing Skills

- Make patterns on the floor with precut shapes.
- Start with one of each shape.
- Let the children add the next shape once they understand the pattern.
- For example, put down one square, one triangle, one square, one triangle, one square, etc.
- Let a child add the next triangle.
- When the children can complete a simple pattern, make more complex ones, for example, two circles, two squares, one triangle; two circles, two squares, one triangle; etc.

Do You Have?

Teaches About Shapes

- Pass out precut circles, squares and triangles to the children.
- Give varying numbers of the different shapes to each child.
- Hold up one circle and ask, "Does anyone have two circles?"
- Children with at least two circles hold them up for all to see.
- Continue with other shapes, changing the named shape and amount.

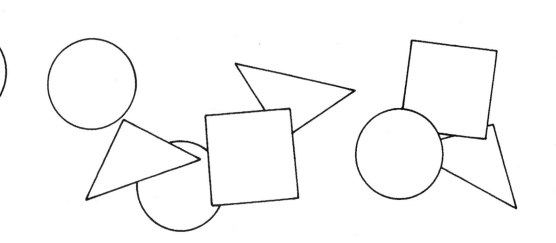

Math Games

Goldilocks

- Recite the following poem with the children.

  When Goldilocks went to the three bears' house

  What did her blue eyes see?

  A bowl that was huge, (make a large circle with arms)

  A bowl that was small, (make a smaller circle with arms)

  A bowl that was teeny and that was all. (make a circle with fingers)

  *She counted them one, two, three. (hold up three fingers one
      at a time)*

- Continue with:

  When Goldilocks went to the three bears' house...

  A chair that was huge...

  When Goldilocks went to the three bears' house...

  A bed that was huge...

  When Goldilocks went to the three bears' house...

  A bear that was huge...

Eensy Weensy Spider

Builds Listening Skills

- This song develops language and listening skills.
- Sing the song all the way through to be sure that the children know the words and the actions that accompany them.
- Explain to them that they are going to sing the song in a new way, but continue making the same movements.
- Here are several ways to sing Eensy Weensy Spider.

    La La La

    Hum

    Whistle

    Beginning letter sounds

    Ooooooo

- Don't sing at all; just perform the actions. You won't believe how quiet children can be!

Let's Travel

Teaches About Transportation

- Talk about different modes of transportation.
- Sing songs about each mode, for example:

    The Wheels on the Bus

    Row, Row, Row Your Boat

    I've Been Working on the Railroad

    She'll Be Coming 'Round the Mountain

Music Games

A New Way

Teaches About Animals

- Sing the song "Old MacDonald Had a Farm."
- Instead of naming the animals, make a sound, for example:

  Old MacDonald had a farm,

  E-I-E-I-O.

  And on his farm he had a _____, (click teeth)

  E-I-E-I-O.

  With a click, click here...etc.

- Sneeze, cough, kiss and make any other sounds that you like.
- Tape-record this version of "Old MacDonald" so that the children can listen and enjoy making the sounds on their own.

In and Out the Village

Develops Coordination

- Stand in a circle and hold hands.
- Sing to the tune of "In and Out the Window."

  Go in and out the village,

  Go in and out the village,

  Go in and out the village,

  As we have done before.

- As you sing, walk into the circle on "in" and walk backward on "out."
- Continue singing other versions.

  Go up and down the village, (hold hands high in the air on "up" and bring them down to the ground on "down")

  Go 'round and 'round the village, (walk in a circle)

- Repeat the first verse.

The Conductor Game

Develops Concentration

- Explain to the children that the conductor of an orchestra tells the other musicians when to play loudly or softly.
- As a sign to play softly, hold both palms in front of your face, facing toward you.
- Place both index fingers on your lips as if to say, "shhh."
- As a sign to play loudly, hold your arms apart, palms toward your face and shake your hands.
- Play instrumental music and use a baton (or a wooden spoon, a rhythm stick, a pencil) to demonstrate as the music becomes louder or softer.
- Try playing this game for five minutes every day.

Musical Ups and Downs

Teaches The Scale

- Sing a major scale. You know it! Do, re, mi, fa, sol, la, ti, do.
- Begin with your body low to the ground and gradually rise as the notes rise.
- When you reach the higher "do," you should be standing on tiptoe with your arms stretched up toward the sky.
- Begin at the higher "do" and move down the scale in the same way.
- Another variation is to go up the scale slowly and come down very fast.

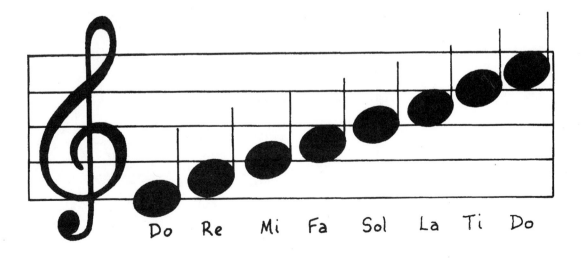

Music Games

Sun Songs

- Color a round paper plate yellow and attach it to a stick.
- Talk about the sun and how it makes you feel.
- Sing songs about the sun.
- Let the children take turns moving the sun back and forth as you sing.
- Sun songs include:

    You Are My Sunshine

    Oh, Mr. Sun

    Sunshine on My Shoulders

- Repeat the game with songs about the moon or stars.
- Star songs include:

    Twinkle, Twinkle, Little Star

    Star Light, Star Bright

    Good Morning, Starshine

    Deep in the Heart of Texas

- Moon songs include:

    Hey Diddle, Diddle

    Oh, Mr. Moon

    Skinnamarinky Dinky Doo

    Fly Me to the Moon

Music Card Box

Teaches The Joy Of Singing

- Make a special box to hold music cards.
- Each time the children learn a new song, create a card with the song's title and a picture related to the song.
- For "Mary Had a Little Lamb," use a picture of a girl with a lamb. For "The Wheels on the Bus," locate a picture of a bus.
- File the card in the music card box.
- Whenever you have a few spare minutes, show the children a card from the music card box.
- Ask them if they know the title of the song on the card.
- Sing the song together.

Little Peter Rabbit

Improves Memory Skills

- Sing this children's song to the tune of "The Battle Hymn of the Republic."

  Little Peter Rabbit had a fly upon his ear.
  Little Peter Rabbit had a fly upon his ear.
  Little Peter Rabbit had a fly upon his ear,
  And he flicked it and it flew away.

- Repeat the song, leaving out the nouns.

  Little Peter Rabbit had a _____ upon his _____, etc.

- Substitute a clap for each noun. Developmentally, this is more difficult than just omitting a word.
- Young children will simply enjoy singing, but older children like the extra challenge of substituting claps for words.

Music Games

Sleigh Ride

Teaches Galloping

- This musical game is a little easier for four and five year olds than younger children.
- Because galloping usually precedes skipping, this game offers good practice for skipping.
- Composer Leroy Anderson wrote a wonderful piece of music called "Sleigh Ride." Play the music for the children and tell them it is about horses pulling a sleigh through the snow.
- Let the children move to the music however they please.
- Then show them how to gallop by placing one foot in front of the other and moving to the music.
- Another wonderful piece of music for this activity is the "Troika" from the "Lieutenant Kije Suite" by Prokofiev.

Bingo

Enhances Listening Skills

- This popular song requires careful thinking and listening.

    There was a farmer had a dog,

    And Bingo was his name, oh.

    B-I-N-G-O, B-I-N-G-O,

    B-I-N-G-O, and

    Bingo was his name, oh.

- Sing the song six times.
- The first time sing all the words.
- Each consecutive time, drop the last letter of "Bingo" and substitute a clap for the letter.
- Think of other animal names with five letters.
- Sing the song the same way using one of those names.

    There was a farmer had a cat,

    And Tabby was her name, oh.

    Tabby... etc.

Music Games

The Lyric Game

Practices Listening Skills

- Choose a song that the children love, for example, "The Wheels on the Bus."
- Make cards with key words from the lyrics like "wheels" and "bus."
- Each time the children sing "wheels," hold up the card that says "wheels."
- Do the same with the word "bus."
- Pictures to illustrate the word on each card will help the children recognize the words faster.

Fleas

Teaches The Diatonic Scale

- Sing this song while crawling your fingers up and down your body. Sing each line on a different note of the scale, beginning with "do" as in do, re, mi, fa, sol, la, ti, do.

  On my toe there (do)
  Is a flea. (re)
  Now he's climbing (mi)
  On my knee, (fa)
  Past my tummy, (sol)
  Past my nose, (la)
  On my head where (ti)
  My hair grows. (do)
  On my head there (stay on do)
  Is a flea. (ti)
  Now he's climbing (la)
  Down on me, (sol)
  Past my tummy, (fa)
  Past my knee, (mi)
  On my toe, (re)
  TAKE THAT YOU FLEA! (tickle your toe)

- This game is also fun with a partner.

Music Games

There's a Cobbler

- Recite this poem with the children.
- Each time you say "bang," the children pretend to hammer a nail into a shoe.

    There's a cobbler down our street

    Mending shoes for little feet

    With a bang and a bang

    And a bang, bang, bang.

    With a bang and a bang

    And a bang, bang, bang.

    Mending shoes the whole day long,

    Mending shoes to make them strong

    With a bang and a bang

    And a bang, bang, bang.

    With a bang and a bang

    And a bang, bang, bang.

Peas Porridge Hot

- Recite this poem with partners.
- Children sit on the floor facing their partners.
- Partners alternate between clapping their own hands together and clapping each other's hands.

    Peas porridge hot,

    Peas porridge cold,

    Peas porridge in the pot,

    Nine days old.

    Some like it hot,

    Some like it cold,

    Some like it in the pot,

    Nine days old.

Music Games

What's the Sound?

Builds Listening Skills

- Sit the children in a circle.
- Choose two rhythm instruments that make different sounds, like a triangle and a maraca.
- Introduce the instruments and play them for the children.
- Ask the children to hide their eyes as you play one of the instruments.
- Ask them to listen and identify which instrument you are playing.
- When this game becomes easy for the children, add a third instrument, a fourth, etc.

An Instrument Story

Develops Listening Skills

- Young children love "Eensy Weensy Spider."
- Accompanying the song with rhythm instruments makes it even more fun and provides a way to teach the concepts of high and low.

> Eensy weensy spider went up the water spout. (go up the scale on a xylophone or hit two rhythm sticks together)
>
> Down came the rain and washed the spider out. (go down the scale on the xylophone or hit two cymbals together)
>
> Out came the sun and dried up all the rain, (hit the triangle)
>
> And the eensy weensy spider went up the spout again. (repeat the first line)

Music Games

Mouth Maracas

Encourages Creative Thinking

- Click your tongue in the back of your mouth to make a sound like a maraca.
- Divide the children into two groups. Let one group sing a song and the other accompany the song by making maraca sounds.
- Switch sides.
- Adapt this same technique to any song the children already know.

Who Is That Singing?

Enhances Listening Skills

- Children enjoy this wonderful listening game.
- Choose two children to come to the front of the room and stand with their backs turned to the others.
- Select one of the two to sing "Mary Had a Little Lamb."
- Do not tell the rest of the children who is singing.
- Ask the children to identify the singer.
- Try this game with three children standing in front.

Pop Goes the Weasel

Improves Listening Skills

- Pass out rhythm sticks or blocks to all the children.
- Sing "Pop Goes the Weasel."
- Ask the children to hit their sticks or blocks together on the word "pop."
- Suggest different ways to hit them together: in the air, loudly or softly, behind your back, under your legs, etc.
- Have the children pretend to hide their sticks. Then, when they sing "pop," have them hit the sticks together high in the air.

Music Games

Mystery Music

- Hum the melody of a familiar song or sing "la, la, la" instead of the words.
- Ask the children to identify the song.
- Repeat the song, stopping on a certain word.
- See if they can identify that word.
- Ask them what the next word of the song would be.

Pussy Willow

Teaches The Scale

- Each line of this poem is sung on a different note of the scale, beginning with "do" as in do, re, mi, fa, sol, la, ti, do.

    I have a little pussy, (do)

    Her fur is silver gray. (re)

    She lives down in the meadow (mi)

    Not very far away. (fa)

    She'll always be a pussy, (sol)

    She'll never be a cat. (la)

    For she's a pussy willow. (ti)

    Now what do you think of that! (do)

    Meow, meow, meow, meow, meow, meow, meow, meow.
    (sing back down the scale, one meow for each note)

    SCAT!!

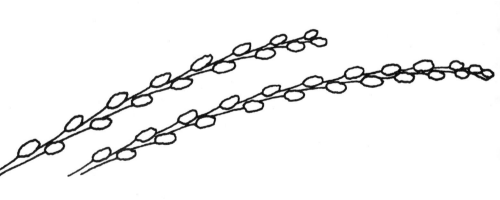

Music Games

Name That Tune

- Sing the melody of a favorite song, substituting "la, la, la" for the words.
- Ask the children to raise their hands as soon as they recognize the melody. This is not easy for preschoolers, who become so excited upon recognizing the melody that they scream out the name.
- Asking the children to raise their hands instead of speaking out helps children who need more time to identify the song.
- Start with songs that you are sure they know, like "Twinkle, Twinkle, Little Star" or "Mary Had a Little Lamb."
- Ask if any children would like to sing a song and have the rest of the class guess its name.

Ring-Around-the-Rosy

Teaches Fun

- This popular circle game is fun for young children and an excellent stress-reliever.
- Let each child select a partner and play the game in pairs.
- Recite the poem, falling down on the word "down." Then say "boom" in a big voice.

    Ring-around-the-rosy

    A pocketful of posies

    Ashes, ashes,

    We all fall down.

    BOOM!

Sing Around the Room

Encourages Creative Thinking

- Think of many different ways to sing a song.

  Sing it fast

  Sing it slowly

  Sing it loudly

  Sing it softly

  Whisper it

  Sing it sitting down

  Sing it standing up

  Sing it standing on one foot

  Sing it lying down

Quartet

Teaches Musical Terms

- Recite this poem.

  One voice is a solo.

  Two is a duet.

  Three voices, a trio.

  Four is a quartet.

  By Jackie Silberg

- Line up four children.
- The first child says, "One voice is a solo."
- The second and first say, "Two is a duet."
- The third, second and first say, "Three voices, a trio."
- The fourth, third, second and first say, "Four is a quartet."
- Ask one child to sing, "Mary Had a Little Lamb."
- Then ask two children to sing it.
- Ask three children to sing.
- Finally, ask four children to sing.
- Observe with the children what happens to music when you continually add more singers.
- Use these terms with the children on other occasions to reinforce the concepts.

Music Games

The Ice Cream Man

Develops Imagination

- Choose one child to be the "ice cream man."
- Sing to the tune of "The Muffin Man" while standing in a circle.

  Oh, do you know the ice cream man,

  The ice cream man, the ice cream man.

  Oh, do you know the ice cream man,

  Who drives the ice cream truck.

- While the children sing, the ice cream man pretends to drive around the circle.
- When the song ends, the ice cream man stops. The child closest to him tells what kind of ice cream she would like.
- Encourage the children to invent unusual kinds of ice cream, like cantaloupe ice cream, peanut butter ice cream, pizza ice cream.

Found a Peanut

Improves Memory Skills

- This never-ending song is a favorite among young children.
- It develops memory skills, and it is great fun to act out.
- Sing to the tune of "Clementine."

  Found a peanut, found a peanut,

  Found a peanut just now.

  I just now found a peanut,

  Found a peanut just now.

Broke it open, broke it open,

Broke it open just now.

I just now broke it open,

Broke it open just now.

It was rotten, it was rotten...

Ate it anyway, ate it anyway...

Got sick, got sick...

Called the doctor, called the doctor...

Appendicitis, appendicitis...

Operation, operation...

Died anyway, died anyway...

Went to heaven, went to heaven...

Walked around, walked around...

Found a peanut, found a peanut...

Oh, When the Band

Teaches About Marching

- Sing to the tune of "When the Saints Come Marching In."

    Oh, when the band,

    Comes marching in,

    Oh, when the band comes marching in,

    I want to march and play in the band,

    When the band comes marching in.

- The children sing and march along while pretending to play an instrument.

- Suggest band instruments such as drums, tuba, piccolo, trombone, etc.

- Someone can twirl a baton.

Music Games

Wheels on the Bus

- This game offers a different way to sing the popular children's song "The Wheels on the Bus."
- Sing it all the way through, acting it out as usual.
- Sing it again, but act out the motions without singing the words.
- For example, do not sing "'round and 'round": just move your hands in a circular motion.
- Continue performing the actions without singing the words.
- This requires a lot of concentration and thinking.

Hum a Tune

Develops Listening Skills

- Ask the children to name several of their favorite songs.
- Select three songs and sing them as a group until everyone is familiar with the melodies.
- Explain to the children that you are going to play a special game. You are going to hum one of the three songs, and you want them to listen and guess which one it is.
- Whoever guesses correctly, hums the next song while the others guess.
- After playing this game a few times, let them hum any song that the class knows.

Matching Tones

Builds Listening Skills

- Invent a simple melody to accompany a group of words. Ask the children to imitate you.
- Sing "Hello, everybody."
- Ask the children to sing exactly as you did.
- Continue singing the same words and melody, but in different ways. Always have the children repeat what you do.
- Try singing loudly, softly, fast and slowly.

Music Games

Little Pine Tree

Practices Language Skills

- Sing to the tune of "I'm a Little Teapot."

    Here's our little pine tree tall and straight.

    Let's find the things so we can decorate.

    First, we want to put a star on top,

    Then we must be careful that the balls don't pop.

    Hang on all the tinsel, shiny and bright.

    Put on the canes and hook them just right.

    Finally, put some presents for you and me,

    And we'll be ready with our Christmas tree.

King Goes 'Round the Village

Teaches Enjoyment Of Music

- Select one child to be king or queen. All the others stand in a circle.
- Everyone sings this song to the tune of "Go In and Out the Window."

    The king goes 'round the village,

    The king goes 'round the village,

    The king goes 'round the village,

    As he has done before.

- The king walks around the circle. As he touches the children, they raise their hands up high in the air.
- At the end of the song, the king closes his eyes and points to a new king or queen, and the game begins again.

Music Games

Greeting Song

- Sing to the tune of "Are You Sleeping?"

    Where is Derek? Where is Derek?

    "Here I am. Here I am." (Derek answers)

    How are you today, sir?

    "Very well, I thank you." (Derek answers)

    Glad you're here, glad you're here. (everyone sings)

- Continue with another child.

Oh, Chester

- This popular camp song is sung to the tune of "Yankee Doodle."

    Oh, Chester (hands on chest)

    Have you heard (hands on ears)

    About Harry? (hands on hair)

    Just got back (hands on chest and then on back)

    From the army. (point to arm and then to yourself)

    I (point to eye)

    Hear (point to ear)

    He knows (point to nose)

    How to wear a rose. (point to your heart)

    Hip, hip, hooray (pat your hips with your hands)

    For the army! (point to arm and then to yourself)

- The song is great fun to sing slowly at first, then with each repetition, speed up.

- This game may be quite difficult for younger children. Five and six year olds will enjoy the challenge.

Music Games

Go Tell Aunt Rhody

Improves Coordination

- Sing "Go Tell Aunt Rhody" with the following words.

    Go tell Aunt Rhody,

    Go tell Aunt Rhody,

    Go tell Aunt Rhody

    That I can walk today.

- Have the children walk around in a circle while they sing.

- Ask a child to choose another movement to do while singing, such as jumping, hopping, skipping, etc.

Twinkle, Twinkle

Teaches Musical Phrasing

- Sing "Twinkle, Twinkle, Little Star" and clap your hands to the syllables.

- Clap for seven beats, and on the eighth beat, keep silent.

- Tell the children to freeze on the eighth beat.

- Twin—kle twin—kle lit—tle star

- clap—clap—clap—clap—clap—clap—clap (freeze)

- How—I won—der what—you are

- clap—clap—clap—clap—clap—clap—clap (freeze)

- Continue the same way with each line.

- Instead of clapping, jump or stamp your feet.

Music Games

The Music Man

Teaches About Musical Instruments

- Gather the children in a circle.
- Start the game by reciting:

    I am the music man,

    I come from far away,

    And I can play.

- The children ask, "What can you play?"

    I can play the trumpet.

    Toot, toot-ti, toot, toot, toot.

- The children repeat, "Toot, toot-ti, toot, toot, toot," all pretending to play the trumpet.
- Follow the same pattern with other instruments and their sounds, for example:

    Drums—boom, boom-di, boom, boom, boom (pretend to beat the drum)

    Violin—la, la-di, la, la, la (pretend to play the violin)

    Flute—tweet, tweet-ti, tweet, tweet, tweet (pretend to play the flute)

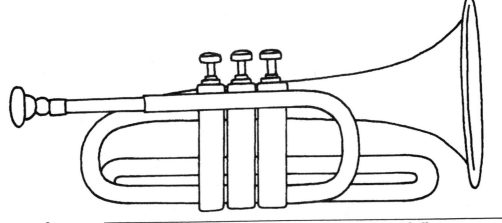

John Brown's Baby

Enhances Listening Skills

- This song is sung to the tune of "Battle Hymn of the Republic."

    John Brown's baby has a cold upon his chest,

    John Brown's baby has a cold upon his chest,

    John Brown's baby has a cold upon his chest,

    And they rubbed it with camphorated oil.

- Sing the first time without any actions.
- The second time, do not sing "baby," but instead rock your folded arms.
- The third time, rock your arms instead of singing "baby" and cough instead of singing "cold."
- The fourth time, rock your arms, cough, and instead of singing "chest," place your hands on your chest.
- The fifth time, rock your arms, cough, place your hands on your chest, and instead of singing "rubbed," rub your chest.
- The sixth time, rock your arms, cough, place your hands on your chest, rub your chest, and instead of singing "camphorated oil," hold your nose.
- This game challenges even older children.

One Finger

Develops Coordination

- This is a popular song that children enjoy very much.
- If you don't know the melody, saying the words is just as much fun.
- Start the song quietly, sitting down.
- The actions build up with each verse. Keep in constant motion throughout the song.

    One finger, one thumb, keep moving
    One finger, one thumb, keep moving
    One finger, one thumb, keep moving
    And we'll all be merry and bright.

    One finger, one thumb, one arm, keep moving...
    One finger, one thumb, one arm, one leg, keep moving...
    One finger, one thumb, one arm, one leg, one nod of the head, keep moving...
    One finger, one thumb, one arm, one leg, one nod of the head, stand up, keep moving...
    One finger, one thumb, one arm, one leg, one nod of the head, stand up, sit down, keep moving...
    One finger, one thumb, one arm, one leg, one nod of the head, stand up, sit down, turn around, keep moving...

- Make up as many additional actions as you wish.

Music Games

This Little Light

Teaches Fun

- Turn off the lights and shine a flashlight in different places around the room.
- Sing "This Little Light of Mine" with the children. On the last line, shine the flashlight on one of the children. Everyone calls out that child's name.

    This little light of mine, I'm gonna let it shine.

    This little light of mine, I'm gonna let it shine.

    This little light of mine, I'm gonna let it shine,

    Let it shine, let it shine, on YOU!

- The child who is "you" shines the flashlight on someone else in the next round.
- NOTE: Never shine a flashlight into anyone's eyes.

Mrs. Macaroni

Teaches Language Skills And Coordination

- Choose one child to be Mr. or Mrs. Macaroni.
- The children form a circle around Mr. or Mrs. Macaroni and skip around singing the following to the tune of "Ten Little Indians."

    Here comes Mrs. Macaroni,

    Riding on her milk-white pony.

    Here she comes with all her money,

    Mrs. Macaroni.

- Mrs. Macaroni chooses a partner.
- The two children skip around the inside of the circle while the others stand in place, clapping their hands.
- Everybody sings:

    Giddiup pony, giddiup pony

    Giddiup pony, giddiup pony,

    Mrs. Macaroni.

- Choose a new Mrs. Macaroni.

Nursery Rhyme Games

Margery Daw

Develops Social Skills

- Seat the children on the floor, facing a partner.
- Partners hold hands, rocking back and forth on an imaginary seesaw. Recite this nursery rhyme as they rock.

> *Seesaw, Margery Daw,*
> *Jackie shall have a new master.*
> *He shall have but a penny a day,*
> *Because he can't work any faster.*
> *(repeat)*

Thinking Game

Practices Memory Skills

- Sit the children in a circle and recite a familiar nursery rhyme. Ask questions about the nursery rhyme's meaning.
- Encourage the children to think about their answers.
- Here are some ideas.

> *For "Little Miss Muffet":*
> *What is a tuffet?*
> *What are curds and whey?*
>
> *For "Old Mother Hubbard":*
> *What is a cupboard?*
> *What else is in the cupboard?*
>
> *For "Little Boy Blue":*
> *Why was Little Boy Blue in the haystack?*
> *Why did he go there?*
>
> *For "Mary Had a Little Lamb":*
> *Where else did Mary go besides school?*
> *Did the lamb follow her to other places?*

Nursery Rhyme Games

Hickory, Dickory

Teaches Rhythm

- Recite "Hickory, Dickory, Dock" with the children, pausing at the end of each line.

  Hickory, dickory, dock, (pause)

  The mouse ran up the clock. (pause)

  The clock struck one and down he come, (pause)

  Hickory, dickory, dock. (pause)

- Ask one child to clap at the end of each line.
- Ask another child to strike a wood block.
- Once the children have played this game, they can take turns clapping or using the wood block or another rhythm instrument to mark the rhythm.

Trot to Boston

Enhances Coordination

- The children form a circle.
- Choose one child to be in the middle.
- While the others recite the nursery rhyme, the child in the middle trots around the inside of the circle.
- On the line "And one for Dicky Dandy," the trotting child chooses another child to come into the circle.

  Trot, trot to Boston town,

  To buy a stick of candy.

  One for you and one for me,

  And one for Dicky Dandy.

- The first child joins the circle. Repeat the game with the new child.

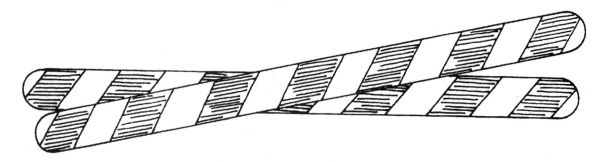

Nursery Rhyme Games

Guess the Song

Teaches Body Awareness

- Pick a popular song that the children enjoy singing like "Twinkle, Twinkle, Little Star."
- Sing the song together.
- Show the children how to "sing" using another part of the body to carry the melody or rhythm, for example:

    Hum

    Click tongue

    Clap hands

    Snap fingers

    Stamp feet

- Try singing the song one of these ways.
- Clap out the rhythm of another familiar song, and see whether the children can identify it.

To Market, To Market

Builds Listening Skills

- Choose one child to be the pig.
- The pig stands at one end of the room.
- Choose another child to go to the market.
- This child stands at the opposite end of the room.
- The others chant the rhyme.

    To market, to market, to buy a fat pig,

    Home again, home again, jiggity jig.

- The child going to the market hops across the room to get the child who is the pig.
- He takes the pig's arm, and together they hop back to the other side of the room.
- Choose two new children to play the game.
- Additional verses include:

    To market, to market, to buy a fat hog,

    Home again, home again, jiggity jog.

    To market, to market, to buy a plum bun,

    Home again, home again, market is done.

Nursery Rhyme Games

Jack Be Nimble

Promotes Coordination

- Place several unlit candlesticks (real or imaginary) around the room.
- Help the children learn "Jack Be Nimble."

    Jack be nimble, Jack be quick,

    Jack jump over the candlestick.

- Choose one child to be "Jack."
- Jack tries to jump over a candlestick while the others recite the rhyme.
- Choose another child to be "Jack."
- Repeat the game with a taller candlestick.

Rhythm Stick Counting

Improves Coordination

- Sing "This Old Man."
- After the end of the first verse, ask the children to clap once.
- Continue with the second verse. At the end, clap twice.
- Clap after each verse. Once you get to three, it is a good idea to count out loud as you clap.

Nursery Rhyme Games

Nursery Rhyme Numbers

Builds Listening Skills

- Every day recite a nursery rhyme whose lyrics include a number.
- The first day, recite rhymes with the number one.
- The next day, recite rhymes with the number two and repeat the rhymes from the first day.

    One—Hickory, Dickory, Dock

    Two—Two Little Dickey Birds

    Three—Three Blind Mice

    Four—This Old Man

    Five—Five Little Chickadees

    Six—Six Little Ducks

Wee Willie Winkie

Teaches About Time

- Recite "Wee Willie Winkie" with the children.

    Wee Willie Winkie runs through the town,

    Upstairs and downstairs in his nightgown.

    Rapping at the windows,

    Crying through the locks,

    Are the children in their beds?

    For now it's eight o'clock.

- Set the hands of a large clock to eight, or draw a picture of a clock with its hands set at eight.
- Choose someone to be "Wee Willie."
- Repeat the rhyme while he acts it out and says the lines "Are the children in their beds? For now it's eight o'clock."
- Move the hands on the clock or draw a new picture.
- Ask the children if they know what the new time is.
- Choose another child to act out the rhyme and say the last line with the new time.

Nursery Rhyme Games

Nursery Rhyme Fun

Develops Number Recognition

- Recite a variety of nursery rhymes and ask the children to listen for numbers.
- Tell them to raise both hands high whenever they hear a number.
- "Hickory, Dickory, Dock" is a good rhyme with which to start.

    Hickory, Dickory, Dock,

    The mouse ran up the clock.

    The clock struck one,

    And down he run.

    Hickory, Dickory, Dock.

- Other nursery rhymes with numbers include:

    One, Two, Buckle My Shoe

    Baa, Baa, Black Sheep

    Three Blind Mice

    Sing a Song of Sixpence

Counting Rhymes

Practices Counting Skills

- Here are familiar counting rhymes with which to pass a few minutes.

    One, two, three, four,

    Mary's at the cottage door.

    Five, six, seven, eight,

    Eating cherries off a plate.

    Five little peas in a pea pod pressed, (curl five fingers into one hand)

    One grew, and two grew, and so did all the rest. (open fingers out)

    They grew and grew and grew and grew

    And grew and never stopped.

    They grew so plump and portly that the pea pod

    POPPED! (clap hands)

Nursery Rhyme Games

One, two, three, four, five,

I caught a fish alive.

Six, seven, eight, nine, ten,

Then I let him go again.

Why did you let him go?

Because he bit my finger so.

Which finger did he bite?

This little finger on the right.

Nursery Rhyme Game

Promotes Language Skills

- Quote lines from favorite nursery rhymes or songs.
- Ask the children to identify the people in the rhymes.
- For example, "Two people I know went up the hill to fetch a pail of water."
- The children will answer "Jack and Jill."
- Here are some other ideas.

    Someone had a little lamb, little lamb, little lamb

    Someone is nimble, he is also quick

    Someone had a farm, E-I-E-I-O

Nursery Rhyme Games

Rhyming Practice

- Making children aware of rhyming takes practice.
- A good way to start is by singing songs that the children already know.
- Stop at the end of a line to let them fill in the word, for example:

    Twinkle, twinkle, little star,

    How I wonder what you _____.

    Yankee Doodle went to town,

    'A riding on his pony.

    Stuck a feather in his cap,

    And called it _____.

- Play this game with the children's favorite nursery rhymes, for example:

    Little Miss Muffet

    Little Boy Blue

    Hickory, Dickory, Dock

Talking Fun

Develops Memory Skills

- Pick a nursery rhyme that the children enjoy.
- First, say the rhyme together to make sure that everyone knows it.
- Next, alternate lines: you say a line, then the children say a line.

    Baa, Baa, Black Sheep, have you any wool?

    Yes, sir, yes, sir, three bags full. (children say this line)

- Continue until the end.
- A variation is to change the sound of your voice as you say the rhyme, and ask the children to repeat the lines in the same manner.

Nursery Rhyme Games

Jack Be Nimble

Develops Safety Skills

- Ask the children to sit in a circle.
- Turn down the lights and light a candle.
- Start speaking:

  Jack be nimble,

  Jack be quick,

  Jack jump over the candlestick.

- Blow out the candle and turn on the lights.
- Talk about the poem.
- Talk about why it would be dangerous to jump over a lit candlestick.
- Explain what the words nimble and quick mean.
- Say the rhyme together and pretend to jump over the candlestick.

Diddle, Diddle, Dumpling

Teaches Fun

- Children love the poem "Diddle, Diddle, Dumpling."
- Explain to them that the word "dumpling" is a term of affection like honey, sweetie, etc.
- Say the rhyme together:

  Diddle, diddle, dumpling,

  My son John.

  Went to bed with his stockings on.

  One shoe off,

  And one shoe on,

  Diddle, diddle, dumpling,

  My son John.

- Recite the poem, changing the beginning consonant of "Diddle, Diddle, Dumpling."

  Biddle, Biddle, Bumpling

  Ziddle, Ziddle, Zumpling

- This is a lot of fun, and children enjoy it very, very much.

Nursery Rhyme Games

Say the Rhyme

Improves Memory Skills

- Print the title of a favorite nursery rhyme on a card.
- Next to the title, place a picture that represents the rhyme. For example, put a picture of a spider next to "Eensy, Weensy Spider."
- Make several cards and file them in a box.
- Invite one child to draw a card out of the box.
- When he has named the rhyme, ask him to say the rhyme by himself or with the others.

On Stage

Encourages Imagination

- Act out the children's favorite nursery rhymes.
- "Little Miss Muffet," "Jack and Jill" and "Mary Had a Little Lamb" are a few simple rhymes that children love to perform.
- Choose two children to be Miss Muffet and the spider, for example. They perform the actions while the other children say the rhyme.
- Even three year olds can easily play this game.

The Restaurant Man

Builds Vocabulary

- Sing the following song to the tune of "Do You Know the Muffin Man?"

    Oh, do you know the restaurant man,

    The restaurant man, the restaurant man.

    Oh, do you know the restaurant man

    Who eats at _____. (the children fill in the blank, naming their favorite restaurant)

    The restaurant man likes to eat,

    Likes to eat, likes to eat.

    The restaurant man likes to eat

    _____ (the children fill in the blank, naming a food)

Pass the Potato

Encourages Social Skills

- Sit down and sing with the children to the tune of "London Bridge Is Falling Down."

    'Round the circle, here it comes,

    Here it comes, here it comes.

    'Round the circle, here it comes,

    Pass the potato.

- As the children sing, they pass a potato from one to another.
- At the end of the rhyme, the child holding the potato pretends to eat it.
- He also tells whether his potato is mashed, fried, boiled, etc.
- Play this game with other foods.

Nursery Rhyme Games

Old Mother Hubbard

Develops Creative Thinking

- This game gives children a chance to spread their creative wings.
- Recite this traditional nursery rhyme.

    Old Mother Hubbard went to the cupboard,

    To get her poor dog a bone.

    When she got there,

    The cupboard was bare,

    And so her poor dog had none.

- After reciting the poem, repeat it, replacing some of the words, for example:

    Old Mother Hubbard went to the cupboard,

    To get her poor dog a _____.

- Let the children fill in the blank with a pizza, a dress, a hat, etc.
- Next, replace the dog with another animal like a giraffe or a hippopotamus, for example:

    To get her poor hippopotamus a banana.

- Have fun with this nursery rhyme.

Hey, Diddle, Diddle

Develops Imagination

- Choose children to play the cat, the cow, the dog, the dish and the spoon.
- Recite the nursery rhyme and act it out.

    Hey, diddle, diddle,

    The cat and the fiddle. (cat pretends to play a fiddle)

    The cow jumped over the moon. (cow jumps)

    The little dog laughed (dog laughs)

    To see such sport,

    And the dish ran away with the spoon. (dish and spoon hold hands and walk away)

- Props add additional fun to acting. You could also use pictures of a cat, fiddle, cow, moon, dog, dish and spoon.

Nursery Rhyme Games

Eat Brown Bread

Promotes Imagination

- This traditional English rhyme is very popular with young children.

  I-tidd-ly-i-ti

  Eat brown bread.

  I saw a sausage

  Fall down dead.

  Up jumped a saveloy

  And bumped him on the head.

  I-tidd-ly-i-ti

  Eat brown bread.

- A saveloy is a spicy dried sausage.
- Have the children pretend to be sausages falling down and jumping up.
- On "brown bread" in the last line, clap loudly twice.

Little Jack Horner

Teaches Imagination

- Children love acting out this nursery rhyme.

  Little Jack Horner

    Sat in a corner,

  Eating his Christmas pie.

    (pretend to eat)

  He put in his thumb,

    (put thumb into pie)

  And pulled out a plum,

    (pull out thumb)

  And said, "What a good

    boy am I!" (look very

    proud)

Relaxing Games

Listen to the Snow

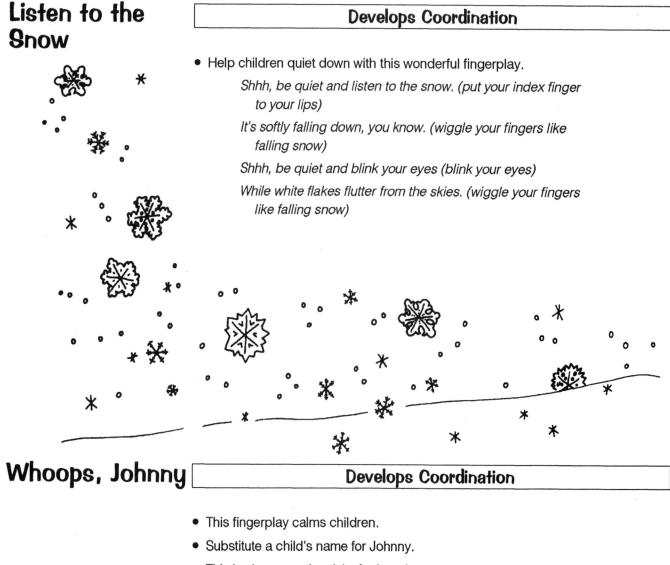

Develops Coordination

- Help children quiet down with this wonderful fingerplay.

    Shhh, be quiet and listen to the snow. (put your index finger to your lips)

    It's softly falling down, you know. (wiggle your fingers like falling snow)

    Shhh, be quiet and blink your eyes (blink your eyes)

    While white flakes flutter from the skies. (wiggle your fingers like falling snow)

Whoops, Johnny

Develops Coordination

- This fingerplay calms children.
- Substitute a child's name for Johnny.
- This is also a good activity for learning names.

    Johnny, Johnny, Johnny, Johnny,

    Whoops, Johnny, whoops Johnny,

    Johnny, Johnny, Johnny.

- Starting with the little finger, touch the fingers one by one on "Johnny."
- On "whoops," slide down the index finger, up the thumb and touch the thumb.
- Then reverse these steps, sliding down the thumb on the second "whoops" and touching the index, middle, ring and little fingers on "Johnny."

Quiet as a Mouse

Practices Listening Skills

- Help children calm down with this poem.

    Can you be so quiet?
    As quiet as a mouse?
    And tippy tippy tippy toe, (tiptoe)
    All around the house?

    Make a quiet circle, (make a circle with arms)
    And quietly sit down.
    Put a smile upon your face, (smile)
    But don't you make a sound.

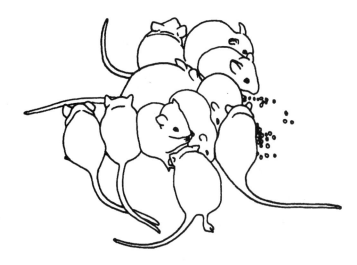

Time to Relax

Teaches Relaxation

- Teach children relaxation techniques to use for a lifetime.
- Lie on the floor.
- Tighten and then relax different parts of the body.
- Start with the toes and work your way up to the head.
- Be sure to remember all the facial muscles, including those around the eyes, neck and mouth.
- When you are finished, ask the children to get up very slowly and walk to the door.
- Try this game with the children, and you will all be amazed how good you feel.

Relaxing Games

Loud and Soft

Teaches About Loud And Soft

- Sing a favorite song several times to be sure that the children know the words.
- Divide the song into two sections. Sing the first section softly and the second section loudly.
- Reverse the order, singing the first section loudly and the second, softly.
- Ending in a soft voice is difficult for young children and will require practice.
- A good song for this game is "Yankee Doodle."

Magic Clay

Develops Creativity

- Pretend to have clay in your hands.
- Pat and roll the clay.
- Show the children what you can do with imaginary clay: roll it, stretch it, knead it and throw it in the air.
- Pass the clay to a child and encourage her to do something with the clay.
- Pass the clay around until every child has had a turn.

Stop and Go

Improves Listening Skills

- Play lively instrumental music.
- Tell the children to dance to the music however they like.
- When the music stops, they must freeze in position. They can start again when the music starts.
- Children love this game.
- To calm children, play this game with soft music.

Relaxing Games

Tap Your Feet

Teaches Rhythm

- This poem offers a nice change of pace, good exercise and practice thinking about parts of the body.

  Hello, feet, (tap the ball of your foot on the floor)
  Let's feel the beat.
  Hello, knees, (bend your knees)
  Zip a dee dee.
  Hello, thigh, (move your leg back and forth)
  My, oh, my.
  Hello, hip, (roll your hips around and around)
  Pip, pip, pip.
  Hello, shoulder, (move your shoulders in a circular motion)
  Get a little older.
  Hello, neck, (stretch your neck)
  Picky, picky, peck.
  Hello, head, (move your head back and forth)
  Go to bed. (lay your head on your shoulder and close your eyes)

  By Jackie Silberg

- Sometimes children like to snore!

Rag Doll 1

Teaches Relaxation

- Stand with your feet shoulder width apart.
- Let your arms hang limp like a rag doll.
- Slowly bend over at the waist until your fingertips touch the floor.
- Stay in this position for a few seconds and try to relax totally.
- Slowly come back up, feeling each part of the body as it straightens: hips, waist, back and shoulders, and finally, the head.
- This is an excellent exercise to do between activities.

Relaxing Games

Roll Your Hands

- This activity quiets children and helps them acquire the concepts of fast and slow.
- Recite all three verses of this poem, the first verse slowly, the second, fast and the third, slowly.

    Roll your hands so slowly,

    As slowly as can be.

    Roll your hands so slowly,

    And fold your arms like me.

    Roll your hands so quickly,

    As quickly as can be.

    Roll your hands so quickly,

    And fold your arms like me.

    Roll your hands so slowly,

    As slowly as can be.

    Roll your hands so slowly,

    And fold your arms like me.

Rag Doll 2

Teaches Relaxation

- Ask the children to lie on their backs on the floor.
- Tell them that each time you name a body part, they are to let it hang limp like a rag doll.
- Start with the toes and work your way up to the head.
- Be sure to include mouth and eyes.
- Playing soft instrumental music in the background will add to the mood.

Relaxing Games

Imaginary Walk

Enhances Imagination

- This is a very good game for developing thinking skills.
- Take an imaginary walk around the block.
- Ask the children to close their eyes and imagine a particular place on the block, for example, a playground, a tree or a house or building.
- Ask the children what sounds they would hear if they were on the playground.
- As they name the sounds, ask them to make the sounds.

Children Are Sleeping

Improves Imagination

- The children lie on the floor and cover their faces while pretending to be asleep.
- Say "The children are sleeping, the children are sleeping, and when they wake up, they will be..." (animals, cars, plants growing, etc.)
- The children pretend to wake up and to be whatever you said.
- Play the game several times.
- At the end of the game, say "When they wake up, they will be children again."

Relaxing Games

Say Goodbye

Develops Creativity

- This is a wonderful game to end the day, quiet and calming for the children and enjoyable for all.
- Recite with the children.

    Say goodbye, say goodbye,

    Say goodbye today.

    Now's the time to say goodbye,

    Until another day.

- Replace the word "say" with other words or gestures for saying goodbye such as nod, wave, shake your head, blow a kiss, etc.

Animal Relaxing

Develops Creativity

- Talk about relaxing and the different ways to relax. Sleep, read a book, listen to music, etc.
- Ask the children to name different animals.
- Let one child pretend to be a dog.
- After the "dog" has barked a little, talk with the children about how dogs relax.
- Ask the child who is pretending to be a dog to show how a dog relaxes (chew on a bone, sleep, rest in the grass, etc.).

Rhyming Games

My Aunt Came Back

- The children repeat every line.

  Oh, my aunt came back

  From Honolulu.

  And she brought with her

  A wooden shoe. (shake foot)

  My aunt came back

  From old Japan.

  And she brought with her

  A waving fan. (imitate a fan waving)

- Additional suggestions:

  ...from Montreal...a woolen shawl (wrap your shawl around your shoulders)

  ...from Buffalo...a boat to row (pretend to row a boat)

  ...from London town...a fine silk gown (pretend to show your gown)

  ...from Washington...some bubble gum (chew gum)

  ...from Halifax...a dog named Max (bark like a dog)

- Ask the children for suggestions.

Time for Rhymes

- Play this game after the children have learned about rhyming.
- Tell the children that you are going to find words that rhyme with "hair."
- Ask questions that describe a rhyming word and let the children guess what the word is.

  A word that rhymes with hair is something you sit on.

  A word that rhymes with hair is a juicy fruit that tastes sweet.

  A word that rhymes with hair is to look at someone for a long time.

- Make up other questions for rhyming words.

Rhyming Games

Animal Rhymes

Builds Language Skills

- The lyrics of an old folk song are an excellent way to begin this game, which helps children practice rhyming words.

    Oh, my cat is red.
    She likes honey on her bread.

    Oh, my dog is blue.
    He likes playing in the glue.

    Oh, my cat is black.
    She likes lying on her back.

    Oh, my dog is ... etc.

- Name another color and find rhymes for it.

Can You Rhyme?

Develops Rhyming Skills

- Rhyming is hard for young children.
- With lots of practice and natural speech development, they will eventually enjoy and understand it.
- Create sentences and accent the words to be rhymed.

    Sit by the TREE and tap your KNEE.
    I bought my CAT a brand new HAT.

- Accept all answers whether they rhyme or not.

Rhyming Games

Name Rhymes

- Make up a rhyme for each child's name.
- Even if the rhyming word doesn't make sense, the children will hear the rhyme.
- Recite the verse for each child.

  What's your name?
  Your name is Bill.
  Bill, Bill
  Walks up the hill.

  What's your name?
  Your name is Denise.
  Denise, Denise,
  We wish you peace.

  What's your name?
  Your name is Jackie.
  Jackie, Jackie,
  Quacky, quacky.

Rhyming Practice

- A wonderful way to help children understand the concept of rhyme is to rhyme the last word of each line in a familiar poem.

  Little boy blue—boo, boo, boo
  Come blow your horn—born, born, born
  The sheep's in the meadow—shadow, shadow, shadow
  The cow's in the corn—born, born, born

- Try this with colors, numbers or the children's names.

Rhyming Games

Silly Rhymes

Develops Language Skills

- Children love silly rhymes. Here are a few.

    Oh, Aunt Miranda, look at your Uncle Jim

    Out in the duck pond, learning how to swim.

    First he does the breaststroke, (do the breaststroke)

    Then he does the side. (do the sidestroke)

    Now he's under the water, (go under water)

    Swimming against the tide. (swim under the water)

    There was an old man with a beard,

    Who said, "It is just as I feared.

    Two owls and a hen,

    Four larks and a wren

    Have all built their nests in my beard."

    Sam, Sam, the dirty old man,

    Washed his face in a frying pan.

    Brushed his hair with a donkey's tail,

    And scratched his tummy with his big toenail.

Down by the Bay

Builds Rhyming Skills

- This is a popular children's song that can be spoken as well as sung.

    Leader—Down by the bay

    Children—Down by the bay

    Leader—Where the watermelons grow

    Children—Where the watermelons grow

    Leader—Back to my home

    Children—Back to my home

    Leader—I dare not go

    Children—I dare not go

    Leader—'Cause if I do

    Children—'Cause if I do

Rhyming Games

Leader—My mother will say

Children—My mother will say

Leader—Did you ever see a cat, sitting on a

Children—(fill in the rhyming word)

Leader—Down by the bay.

Children—Down by the bay.

- For example:

    cat sitting on a hat

    dog riding a hog

    snake eating a cake

    bear combing his hair

- Make up your own rhymes.

Name That Rhyme

Improves Listening Skills

- This is an excellent game to help children understand rhyming and to listen to sounds.
- Say rhymes and poems with children that they already know.
- Repeat the poem, leaving out the last word of each line.
- Let the children fill them in.
- For example:

    Teddy bear, teddy bear turn _____.(around)

    Teddy bear, teddy bear touch the _____. (ground)

    Teddy bear, teddy bear tie your _____.(shoes)

    Teddy bear, teddy bear, read the _____.(news)

    Teddy bear, teddy bear, go _____.(upstairs)

    Teddy bear, teddy bear, say your _____.(prayers)

    Teddy bear, teddy bear, turn off the _____.(light)

    Teddy bear, Teddy bear, say _____.(goodnight)

Science Games

Hot and Cold

Teaches About Hot And Cold

- Fill two paper cups, one with hot water, one with cold.
- Let the children put their hands on the outside of the cups.
- Ask them to choose which is hot and which is cold.
- Mark the cups with a red sticker dot for hot and a blue sticker dot for cold.

Where's the Water?

Teaches About Evaporation

- Fill a glass with water.
- Explain to the children that each day they will mark the water level in the glass.
- As days pass, discuss why the mark gets lower and lower.
- What is happening to the water?

Thermometer

Teaches How A Thermometer Works

- Show the children a thermometer.
- Explain how it works.
- Place two bowls on a table.
- Fill each half way, one with cold water and one with warm water.
- Place an outdoor thermometer in one of the bowls.
- Let the children read the temperature.
- Transfer the thermometer to the other bowl and read the temperature again. Observe how the temperature goes up and down.

Science Games

Ice Cube Games

Teaches About Melting

- Try melting an ice cube in different ways.
- Put three ice cubes in separate dishes.
- Allow one to melt by itself, turn a hair dryer on the second and pour hot water on the third.
- Keep track of how long each one takes to melt.
- The class may wish to observe the project three different times over the course of one day.
- Look at them under a magnifying glass.

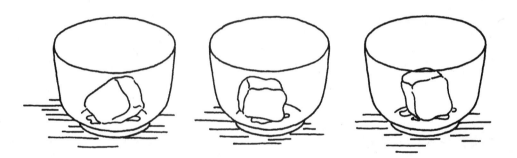

What If?

Develops Critical Thinking Skills

- Ask the children "What if" questions.

  What if the sun stopped shining?

  What if all the water in the ocean dried up?

- Encourage discussion about these questions.

Rising Bubbles

Teaches About Air

- Blow bubbles and shake the wand over a warm floor radiator.
- What a wonderful discovery!
- The bubbles will rise as though they were hot air balloons.

Science Games

Warm and Cold Hands

Teaches About Hot And Cold

- Fill three bowls with cold water, lukewarm water and hot water.

- Let one child put his hand into the cold water and describe how it feels. Ask the child to leave his hand in the cold water and to put his other hand into the warm water and describe how it feels.

- Now ask the same child to put both hands in the lukewarm water and describe how they feel. The hand that was in the cold water should feel warm and the hand that was in the warm water should feel cold.

Catch the Falling Snow

Teaches About Melting

- Set a shallow pan outside on a snowy day to catch the falling snow. Bring the pan inside and watch the snow melt into water.

- Catch snowflakes on dark construction paper.

Paper Science

Teaches About Gravity

- Take two identical sheets of paper.

- Show the children that they are exactly the same.

- Ask a child to crumple up one sheet of paper.

- Drop both sheets of paper, the crumpled one and the uncrumpled one, to the floor from the same height.

- Discuss why one fell faster than the other one.

Science Games

A Juicy Trick

Teaches About Air

- This is a good activity for snack time.
- Punch one hole in a juice can.
- Pour out a little juice.
- Show the children how difficult it is to pour the juice.
- Punch a second hole in the juice can.
- Show the children that the juice pours more easily, and explain that it is because you let more air into the can.

Move That Air!

Teaches About Vibrations

- Explain to the children that sound is made when air moves.
- The movement is called vibration.
- Ask the children to touch their hands to their throats and hum.
- Feel the vibration.
- Explain to the children that their throats contain vocal cords that move back and forth when they talk.
- When they hum, they can feel the vocal cords moving back and forth.
- Another game is to hold the palm of one hand in front of your face.
- Blow on the palm.
- While blowing, move the index finger of your other hand through the air flow.
- Listen to the sound change.

Science Games

Watch the Eggs

Teaches About Water

- Fill two identical glasses with water.
- Add about four tablespoons of salt to one glass.
- Stir the water until it is clear.
- Tell the children to watch what happens next.
- Place one shelled, hard-boiled egg in each glass of water.
- The egg in the glass of unsalted water sinks to the bottom.
- The egg in the saltwater floats.
- It is fun to ask the children, before you put the egg into the unsalted water, if they think the egg will sink to the bottom.
- Ask the question again, before putting the egg into the saltwater, and watch how surprised they are to see that egg float.

Sound Experiments

Teaches About Sound

- Children are fascinated by this experiment.
- Tie a six-inch length of string from each of the two corners of a wire coat hanger.
- Hold the ends of the string, one in each hand.
- Wrap the ends around your index fingers a couple of times.
- Put your index fingers in your ears.
- With the coat hanger dangling, walk around the room, allowing the coat hanger to bump into things made of wood, metal, etc.
- The sounds you hear will be very loud.
- NOTE: For safety reasons, bend the hook of the coat hanger out of the way.

Water Day

Teaches About Water

- This game helps children realize the importance of water.
- Obtain a large container and a small measuring cup.
- Ask the children how they use water.

- Every time a new use is mentioned, fill the small cup with water and pour it into the large container.
- The children will probably mention drinking water, washing hands, flushing a toilet, feeding animals, watering plants and cooking.
- The large container, full of water, offers a visual lesson in water's importance.
- After the container is full, water the classroom plants with it.

Bones

Teaches About Bones

- This game has two parts, carried out several days apart.
- Clean a chicken bone carefully.
- Let the children feel the bone and then feel their own bones.
- Talk about what bones do and why they are important. Talk about calcium in the bones and how that makes them strong.
- Soak the chicken bone in vinegar for several days.
- Vinegar takes calcium out of the bones and so weakens them.
- After several days, remove the bone.
- The bone will bend easily.
- Let the children feel it again.
- Ask them what happens to bones when the calcium is gone.

If I...

Teaches About Cause And Effect

- Help the children think about cause and effect.
- Begin a sentence with "If I..."
- Encourage the children to think of possible outcomes, for example:

    If I water the flowers, they will grow.

    If I pick up my toys...

    If I go outside without a coat...

    If I go to bed with my clothes on...

    If I turn on the hot water...

Science Games

The Mystery Food

- Place an apple in the bottom of a coffee can.
- Cover the can by stretching a sock over the top.
- Let the children reach into the can, with the sock covering their hand.
- Ask them to identify the fruit or vegetable inside the can by feeling it.
- Ask questions like "Is it rough?" "Is it smooth?"
- Ask each child not to tell what they think the object is until all the children have had a turn to feel what is inside the can.
- Try oranges, peppers, zucchini and bananas.

Feel the Glass

Develops Sensory Awareness

- Fill two glasses, one with hot water and one with ice water.
- Let the children feel the glasses and describe which is hot and which is cold.
- Blindfold one child at a time and let him touch one of the glasses.
- He can touch it with his hands first, then try placing it next to his face.
- NOTE: Be sure the water is not so hot it could scald a child.
- This is a great game for developing language about how things feel.

Plant a Little Seed

Teaches About Growth

- Act out the following poem.

  Dig a little hole.
  Plant a little seed.
  Pour on a little water.
  Pull a little weed.

  Give a little sunshine,
  And before you know,
  Your little seed will be a plant,
  And grow, grow, grow.

  Flowers, flowers, flowers,
  Hurry up, hurry up.
  Flowers, flowers, flowers,
  Grow, Grow, Grow.

Making Thunder

Builds Scientific Understanding

- Blow a paper bag full of air.
- Tie the bag closed with a string.
- Place one hand on the top and the other hand on the bottom of the bag.
- Quickly push your hands together, and the bag will pop as it opens.
- Fast-moving air makes a sound.
- Reinforce this activity with a rain poem like "Rain, Rain, Go Away."

Science Games

Food Surprise

- Fill small ziplock bags with dry cereal.
- Pass out one bag to each child.
- Tell the children to crush the cereal in the bag.
- Open the bags one by one, and place a magnet near the crushed cereal. Watch as iron filings attach to the magnet.
- This experiment offers a very impressive visual explanation of food additives!

Seeds

- Try this poem to reinforce a discussion about planting.

    I work in my garden,

    I plant seeds in a row.

    The rain and the sunshine

    Will help my seeds grow.

    Sometimes the weather

    Is dry and hot,

    So I sprinkle the earth

    With my watering pot.

    The roots push downward,

    The stems push up,

    Soon I will see a buttercup.

Science Games

Make a Rainbow
| Teaches About Light Reflection |

- Fill a large, deep, clear dish or glass with water.
- Be sure the water is motionless.
- Put a mirror into the water at an angle so that sunlight goes through the water and reflects off the mirror.
- Look at the wall where the mirror has projected a beam of sunlight making a rainbow!

Making Clouds
| Teaches About Condensation |

- Fill a large glass jar with hot water.
- Pour out all the water except for about an inch.
- As soon as you pour off the water, wrap a cloth over the mouth of the jar.
- Put some ice on top of the cloth.
- Soon a cloud will form in the jar above the water.
- NOTE: The water must be very, very hot when you pour it out, so use great caution around young children. Be sure to leave no more than an inch of hot water in the glass. The cloth should be thin enough that the ice easily melts.

A Magical Balloon
| Teaches About Carbon Dioxide |

Soda bottle

balloon with 2 Ts. baking soda inside

¼ cup vinegar

- Pour 1/4 cup vinegar into a glass bottle. A soda bottle works well.
- Put two tablespoons of baking soda into a balloon.
- Attach the balloon to the neck of the bottle, leaving the balloon hanging limply alongside.
- Tell the children that the balloon will blow up all by itself.
- Hold the balloon up straight, letting the baking soda fall directly into the vinegar.
- Carbon dioxide gas will form and fill the balloon, expanding it.
- Be prepared for lots of "oohs" and "aahs" and many questions.

Science Games

Moving Things with Air

Teaches About Air

- Show the children how to blow through straws held in their mouths.
- Tell them to put their hands in front of the other end of the straw and feel the air blowing out.
- Set lightweight balls like ping-pong balls on a table and show the children how to move the balls by blowing on them.
- Experiment with other objects and see if the children can move them by blowing on them.

It's in the Bag

Teaches About Air

- Show the children a small, empty paper bag.
- Pass it around, allowing the children to insert their hands into the bag to confirm that nothing is inside.
- Tell the children that even though the bag is empty, there is something inside it.
- Gather the bag at the top, leaving just a little opening.
- Have one child blow into the bag. Tie it closed with string.
- Pass the bag around again and ask whether it feels as if something is inside the bag.
- This is a good experiment for demonstrating that although you cannot see air, it takes up space.

Rocks, Rocks, Rocks

Teaches About Hard And Soft

- This is a good, quick game to play outside.
- It gives the children a chance to experience texture.
- Find three or four rocks.
- Scratch the rocks with your fingernails.
- Decide if the rocks are hard or soft.
- Ask the children to find more hard and soft rocks.

I Can Feel the Rhythm

Develops Body Awareness

- Ask the children to try to find their heartbeat.
- Listen very carefully.
- Ask them to find their pulse.
- The pulse is easiest to find in the right side of the neck.
- Have everyone run in place for about twenty seconds.
- Check your heartbeat and pulse again and notice the difference.
- Here's a nice poem about the heartbeat.

> *I can feel the rhythm of my heart, oh, baby,*
> *I can feel the rhythm of my heart. (find heartbeat)*
> *I can feel the rhythm of my pulse, oh, honey,*
> *I can feel the rhythm of my pulse. (find pulse)*
>
> *By Jackie Silberg*

People Magnets

Teaches About Magnets

- With the children sitting down, ask them to make believe that one of their hands is a magnet, and the rest of their body is magnetized.

  What happens when you bring the magnet to your knee?

  ...to your foot?

  ...to your head?

- The children will enjoy becoming magnets, and they will better understand how magnets work.

Science Games

Magnets

Teaches About Magnets

- Choose a child to be the magnet.
- Ask her to stand in front of the group.
- The other children come up one at a time and tell the magnet what they are made of.
- If the other child is metal, the magnet places her arms on the child's shoulders and says, "I stick."
- If the child is not metal, the magnet places her arms on the child's shoulders, then removes them, saying, "I don't stick."
- Let each child decide what they are made of.

Bend and Stretch

Builds Science Vocabulary

- This popular action rhyme is an excellent way to introduce the names of the planets.
- After the children have learned the rhyme, talk about the planets.

    Bend and stretch,

    Reach for the stars.
        (bend down, then stretch up high on tiptoes)

    There goes Jupiter,

    Here comes Mars.

    Bend and stretch,

    Reach for the sky.

    Stand on your tiptoes,

- High, high, high.

The Thirsty Flower

Teaches About The Importance Of Water

- After discussing with the children how water helps grass and flowers grow, recite this poem with the children.

> *Here is a thirsty flower.*
> *(cup hands together)*
>
> *See the petals go to sleep.*
> *(fold fingers inward)*
>
> *Down comes the gentle rain and doesn't make a peep.*
> *(move fingers up and down as if the rain were falling)*
>
> *The flower opens up to catch the falling drops,*
> *(open up cupped hands)*
>
> *And drinks the gentle rain and never, never stops.*

Dinosaurs

Teaches The Names Of Dinosaurs

- Recite this chant with the children.

> *Dinosaurs, dinosaurs,*
> *Lived so long ago.*
> *There were many different kinds,*
> *What are some you know?*

- Ask one child to name a dinosaur. Insert her answer into the chant.

> *Brontosaurus, Brontosaurus,*
> *Lived so long ago.*
> *There were many different kinds,*
> *What are some you know?*

- Continue asking the children for new names to use in the chant.

Thinking Games

Detective

- Ask three or four children to stand in front of the others.
- Tell the children that one of those standing is the mystery person.
- Give the children clues to help them figure out who the mystery person is.
- Begin with descriptive clues like hair color, clothing, etc.
- If any clues do not match one of those standing, the children can ask him to sit down. For example, if you say that the mystery person is wearing brown shoes, any standing child not wearing brown shoes, sits down.
- As the children's observation skills develop, ask a larger group to stand in front.

Button Fun

Teaches Cooperation

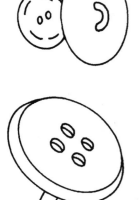

- Save buttons of various colors and sizes in a container.
- Tell the children to each choose a button.
- Ask the children to compare buttons to decide who has the biggest.
- Then identify the next biggest, etc.
- Suggest other classifications for the children to try.

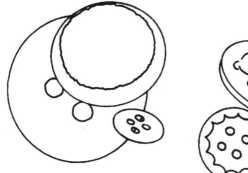
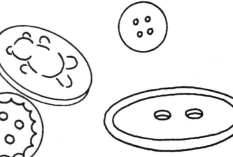

Hard Thinking

- Pose questions to the children to make them think about what happens before or after events.

  Why does Andre put on his snowsuit before he goes outside?

  Where is Laticia going with her shovel?

  Where is the fire truck going?

- Questions can stimulate a wonderful discussion.

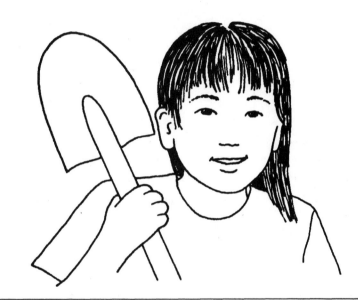

Spatial Concepts

Teaches How To Follow Directions

- Sit the children in a circle with a chair in the middle.
- Choose one child to go to the middle and follow directions.

  Stand behind the chair

  Sit on the chair

  Climb over the chair

  Stand in front of the chair

  Lie under the chair

  Hop around the chair

- Make up more directions with the children.

Thinking Games

The Question Game

Improves Listening Skills

- Ask the children questions and tell them to respond either "yes" or "no."
- Ask silly questions, easy questions and questions that require thinking.
- Here are a few questions to try.

    Does ice cream taste good?

    Is a tomato purple?

    Do tigers wear dresses?

- Pictures of ice cream, tomatoes or tigers make the game a little easier for very young children.

Can You Find It?

Builds Observation Skills

- Lay five objects out on a table in front of the children. Choose recognizable objects like a crayon, a paintbrush, etc.
- Name each object to be sure that all the children know the names.
- Ask the children to cover their eyes as you remove one object.
- Ask them to tell you which object is missing.
- Repeat the game but remove two objects.
- Rearrange the objects and repeat the game again.

True or False

Improves Observation Skills

- Make statements about the children or the room.
- Ask the children to answer "true" if the statement is correct, and "false" if it is incorrect.
- Examples of statements are:

    All the girls are wearing red.

    All the boys are wearing shoes.

    This room has one window.

    Monica is standing on her head.

What's Missing?

Enhances Observation Skills

- Prepare several pictures in advance of objects familiar to the children. Cut them out from magazines, catalogs and old books.
- Cut away one part of the object, for example:

    a car missing a wheel

    a tree missing a trunk

    a spoon missing a handle

    a stuffed animal missing a tail

- You will ask the children to guess what is missing.

Moving Game

Teaches About Slow And Fast, Low And High

- Have the children walk around the room very slowly.
- Increase the speed until they are running.
- Slow down gradually until they are walking at the same speed at which they began.
- Another game teaches the concepts of low and high: ask the children to hold their arms straight down, then slowly lift them higher and higher.
- When their arms are as high as they can reach, tell them to lower their arms very slowly.
- These games help children internalize the concepts of slow to fast and low to high.

Thinking Games

Tiny

Teaches The Concept Of Tiny

- Show the children large and small versions of similar objects, for example, large and small balls, large and small blocks.
- Allow the children to compare the objects.
- Introduce the word "tiny."
- Show the children tiny things, for example, doll house furniture, miniatures of other kinds, etc.
- Talk in a tiny voice (very, very softly).
- Sing familiar songs in a tiny voice.
- Songs to sing include:

    London Bridge Is Falling Down

    Mary Had a Little Lamb

    Twinkle, Twinkle, Little Star

The Senses Game

Builds Sensory Awareness

- Prepare pictures of objects appreciated through the senses. For example, a picture of a flower suggests the senses of smell and sight. A picture of a school bus suggests the senses of hearing and sight.
- Show the pictures to the children.
- Ask questions about the pictures to elicit answers involving one of the senses.

    How do we smell flowers?

    How can we see flowers?

    How can we see the school bus?

    How can we hear the school bus?

Yesterday, Today, Tomorrow

Develops Memory Skills

- Children often confuse "yesterday," "today" and "tomorrow."
- It often helps them to talk about what they did yesterday, what they are doing today and what they will do tomorrow.
- Name three or four things that they did yesterday, for example, finger-painted, baked cookies and played monster.
- Sing these activities to a familiar melody like "Mary Had a Little Lamb," also a good choice because it allows you to list three things.

    Yesterday we finger-painted,

    Baked some cookies,

    And played monster.

    Yesterday we had such fun,

    Let's do it again.

- Then sing about today and tomorrow.
- The following day, be sure to sing about the same activities for "yesterday," that you sang about the day before for "today."
- By repeating this game over time, you will help the children acquire a better understanding of the concepts of yesterday, today and tomorrow.

Thinking Movements

Develops Concentration

- Ask the children to sit perfectly still.
- As they sit, ask each child to think about touching his elbow to his nose.
- Remind them just to think about the movement, not to do it.
- Here are other ideas for "thinking" movements.

    Touch your knee to your ear.

    Touch your chin to your stomach.

    Stand on your head.

    Balance yourself on one knee and one elbow.

- Young children may have difficulty just thinking about a movement. Let them try the movement first, and then just think about it.

Thinking Games

Before and After

- For this game, prepare pictures in advance representing before and after situations, for example:

    A banana and a peeled banana

    A plate with food and an empty plate

    A full glass and an empty glass

    An empty tabletop and a full tabletop

    A messy room and a neat and clean room

- Show the children one picture and ask them what they think happened before or after the picture.
- For example, show the picture of the peeled banana and ask what happened before or after it.
- What happened before, might be that the banana had a peel.
- Show the picture of the unpeeled banana.
- What happened after, might be that the banana was cut into little pieces and put on cereal.
- Continue with other pictures.

Advertising

Promotes Creative Thinking

- Show the children advertisements from magazines or newspapers.
- Ask them what the picture is selling.
- Advertisements for cars, food, toys and clothing are good to begin with.

Thinking Games

How Many?

Enhances Critical Thinking

- Ask questions to expand the children's thinking.

  How many ways can you talk to a friend?

  How many ways can you play outside?

  How many ways can you cook a potato?

  How many ways can you dance to music?

Hand Puppets

Encourages Thinking Skills

- Pretend that one of your hands is a puppet, and the other hand makes the puppet move.
- Pretend that the other hand pulls imaginary strings to make the puppet lift up.
- Wiggle each finger on the puppet hand while the other hand pulls the strings.
- Try moving the puppet hand in many directions.
- Remember that the hand controlling the strings never touches the puppet hand.
- Show very young children a puppet before trying this game.

A Different Simon

Develops Listening Skills

- Play "Simon Says" with the children to be sure that everyone knows how to play the game.
- Tell the children to listen to the directions and follow them. Tell them that you are going to try to trick them by doing something different.
- Their assignment is to follow the directions that you give.
- For example, "Simon says put your hands on your head." The children will put their hands on their head, but you put your hands on your knees.
- This game requires a lot of thinking skill.

Thinking Games

This Is My Right Hand

Teaches About Right And Left

- Recite the poem and perform the actions with the children.

  This is my right hand,

  I raise it up high. (raise your right hand)

  This is my left hand,

  I'll touch the sky. (raise your left hand)

  Right hand, (raise your right hand)

  Left hand, (raise your left hand)

  Whirl them around. (make circles in the air with both hands)

  Right hand, (raise your right hand)

  Left hand, (raise your left hand)

  Pound, pound, pound. (pound your thighs with your fists)

Right Hand Up

Teaches About Left And Right

- Sing the song to the tune of "Jimmy Crack Corn" and perform the actions.

  Right hand up and I don't care,

  Right hand up and I don't care,

  Right hand up and I don't care,

  I put my right hand up.

  Left hand up and I don't care...etc.

  Both hands up and I don't care...etc.

Sound Stories

- Make up a short story and let the children create sounds and movements to go with the story, for example:

    Once there was a little boy who was walking down the street (the children start walking). He stopped (the children stop) and he sneezed (the children sneeze). He heard a bell ringing (make a bell sound), and he thought he'd better run home for dinner (children run in place).

- These stories are a lot of fun. The children will want to do them often.

Transition Games

Jump Three Times

Teaches Jumping

- This is a good game for bridging from one activity to the next.
- Ask the children to stand in a circle.
- Tell them that when their turn comes, they should jump three times and count out loud as they jump.
- Demonstrate how to do this.
- When they are finished jumping, they may go to...(the next activity).

Time for Quiet

Develops Observation Skills

- To end one activity and prepare for another, you need to get everyone's attention.
- Here's a game to settle the children down.
- Ask one child to put his index finger to his lips and signal the next person to do the same.
- Soon everyone will have their fingers on their lips, and the group will be quiet.

Transition

Teaches Friendship Skills

- This chant is a good way to end an activity, leaving everyone feeling good.

    And now it's time to stop,

    But just before we do,

    Everybody join your hands,

    And squeeze a hug to you.

How Do I Get There?

Builds Thinking Skills

- Before leaving to go outside or to another room, talk with the children about the different ways to get there.
- Ask the children if there is more than one way to go outside.
- After discussing the various routes, try one way that day and another the next day.
- Or ask another adult to take a few children one way, while you accompany the others another way.

Important Information

Improves Memory Skills

- Use the time between activities to review the children's addresses and phone numbers.
- Prepare an index card for each child with name, address and phone number.
- File the cards in a box.
- Draw a card.
- Ask the child whose card you drew to say her address, phone number or both.
- This game also helps you identify any child who does not know this information.

Here Come the Robots

Practices Creative Thinking

- Play a robot game.
- The children pretend to be robots and move their bodies accordingly.
- Pretend their arms and legs make sounds.
- Talk like robots and invent conversations.
- This game offers a good transition from one activity to another.

Transition Games

Twiddle Your Thumbs

Promotes Coordination

- This is a great transition fingerplay, which helps children quiet down.
- Recite the poem and carry out the actions.

  You twiddle your thumbs
  And clap your hands,
  And then you stamp your feet.

  You turn to the left,
  You turn to the right,
  And make your fingers meet.

  You make a bridge,
  You make an arch,
  You give another clap.

  You wave your hands,
  You fold your hands,
  And put them in your lap.

Moving with a Smile

Teaches About Feelings

- This good transition game combines movement and feelings.
- Think of all the movements that children can do.
- Ask them to perform an action with a particular emotion.
- Here are some ideas.

  Run with a smile
  Crawl with a hum
  Jump with a sneeze
  Tiptoe with a cough
  March with a laugh

Transition Games

Partner Moves

Improves Coordination

- This is a good transition activity, which also promotes social skills.
- Ask the children to think of ways to move to another part of the room with a friend.

  Holding hands facing forward

  Holding hands facing backward

  Holding hands with one forward and one backward

  Sitting on the floor scooting

  Lying on the floor swimming

  Hopping, jumping or skipping

Transition Time

Builds Classification Skills

- Transition times offer excellent opportunities to reinforce classification skills.

  If you have on brown shoes, you may wash your hands.

  If you are wearing red, you may color.

- Think of other ways to move children from one activity to another by practicing classification, for example:

  ...have brown hair...

  ...are wearing white sneakers...

  ...like to eat bananas...

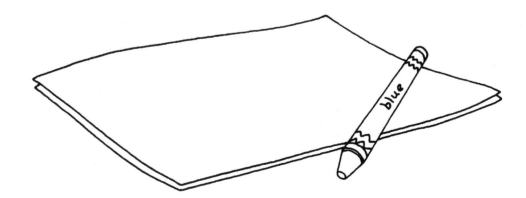

Transition Games

Silent Songs

Develops Listening Skills

- This is a wonderful game when the children are lined up to go somewhere, and you need their attention.

    Mouth the words to a favorite song or fingerplay. Soon everyone will be quiet, mouthing the words with you.

A Name Game

Improves Letter Recognition

- This game is a good way to move children from one activity to another and gives them practice in recognizing letters.
- Go around the room asking each child her name and the letter with which it begins.
- As each child says the initial letter, write it on a sheet of paper, chalkboard or easel.
- Then say to the children, "If your name begins with M, you may go wash your hands."
- Younger children will need help to recognize the letter with which their name begins.

Transition Games

Buzzing Bees

Enhances Imagination

- Cleanup time can be very frustrating.
- Tell the children to pretend to be buzzing bees cleaning up the room.
- Buzz around and pick up things.
- Before long, the hive will be neat and tidy.
- Buzzing bees can also help the children move from one activity to another.
- Buzz to the door when it is time to leave, or buzz to the bathroom when it is time for washing hands.
- Play the music "Flight of the Bumblebee," by Rimsky Korsakoff while the children buzz around.

Ways to Say Goodbye

Practices Language Skills

- There are many ways to say goodbye.
- This is a fun activity with children.
- Select two children at a time. Have them stand facing each other. When they say goodbye, they walk to opposite sides of the room.
- Here are some ideas. Add your own as well.

    Shake hands and say "goodbye"
    Wave goodbye
    Hug each other
    Say "See you later"
    Say "Adios" (Spanish)
    Say "Ta Ta" (English)

End of the Day

Develops Memory Skills

- At the end of the day, help the children remember what they have done during the day.
- Ask them to tell you something that they liked or something that they learned.
- This game strikes a very positive note on which to send the children home.

Weather Games

Walking in the Weather

- Use this poem to develop children's vocabulary about the weather.

  I went for a walk to school today,

  I met the rain and what did it say? (pitter, patter)

  I went for a walk to school today,

  I met the hail and what did it say? (boing, boing)

- Continue the poem introducing sleet, snow, wind or any other weather condition.

Seasonal Playing

- Collect several pictures of children playing in different seasons: swimming, rolling in the snow, etc. Magazines are a good source.

- Whenever you have a few extra minutes, show the pictures to the children and ask them to name the season portrayed.

Weather Games

Clothes Conversation

Seasonal Sounds

Teaches About The Weather

- Show the children three kinds of clothing, for example, a boot, a heavy jacket and a hat.
- Show one article of clothing at a time and talk about why people wear it.
- Ask if they have ever been cold or wet, and what kind of clothing they would have liked to have put on.

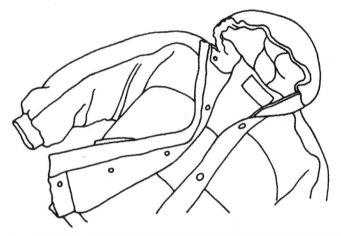

Teaches Weather Vocabulary

- Divide the children into two groups.

  Group One says, "Wintertime, wintertime, cold winds, cold winds."

  Group Two says, "Brrr, brrr, brrr, brrr."

- Repeat for the other seasons.
- Spring

  Group One: "Springtime, springtime, chirping birds, chirping birds."

  Group Two: "Chirp, chirp, tweet, tweet, chirp, chirp, tweet, tweet."

- Summer

  Group One: "Summertime, summertime, hot sun, hot sun."

  Group Two: "Water, water, I want water, water, water, I want water."

- Fall

  Group One: "Now it's fall, now it's fall, rustling leaves, rustling leaves."

  Group Two: "Rustle, rustle, crunch, crunch, rustle, rustle, crunch, crunch."

Weather Games

The March Wind

Encourages Creativity

- Play a March wind game.
- The children form a circle and pretend that they are trees.
- Each child can be a different kind of tree.
- Ask the children what kind of tree they are.
- Choose one child to be the wind.
- The wind rushes in and out of the trees making a sound like blowing wind.
- The trees bend back and forth in the blowing wind.
- At a signal, the wind stops and trades places with a tree.
- The child who was a tree becomes the wind, and the game continues.

Acting Out the Weather

Teaches Body Awareness

- This creative game involves sounds made with hands and feet.
- Teach it to children once, and they will ask to play it again and again.
- Chant:

    Rain, rain, go away,

    Come again another day.

    Everybody wants to play.

- Then perform the following actions in order.

    Make soft raindrops—snap fingers

    Make louder raindrops—snap fingers louder and faster

    Make very loud raindrops—hit hands on thighs

    Make thunder—stamp feet

    Make lightning—clap hands sharply

    Make thunder—see above

    Make very loud raindrops—see above

    Make louder raindrops—see above

    Make soft raindrops—see above

- Repeat the chant in a very soft voice.

Rain

Develops Memory Skills

- This is an echo poem. One group says the words in a normal voice, and the second group repeats the words in a softer voice.

  Rain, rain, (repeat)

  Falling from the sky. (repeat)

  Pitter, patter, (repeat)

  Ooops, it hit my eye. (repeat)

  Rain, rain, (continue repeating each line)

  Falling on my toys.

  Boom, boom, boom, boom,

  Scary sounding noise.

  Rain, rain, (continue repeating each line)

  Falling on my nose.

  Drip, drip, drip, drip,

  Squishing through my toes.

  By Jackie Silberg

- Talk about rain. Where does it come from? What are thunder and lightning?

Rain Sayings

Builds Weather Vocabulary

- Poems are a wonderful way to increase children's vocabulary.

  Pitter, patter, pitter, patter,

  Listen to the rain.

  Pitter, patter, pitter, patter,

  On my windowpane.

  Evening red and morning gray

  Are the signs of a bonny day.

  Evening gray and morning red

  Bring down rain on the farmer's head.

Weather Games

It Rained a Mist

Develops Coordination

- This poem is an American folk song, which is wonderful to act out.

  It rained a mist, it rained a mist,

  It rained all over the town, town, town.

  It rained all over the town. (children wiggle their fingers like
  falling rain)

  The sun came out, the sun came out,

  It shone all over the town, town, town.

  It shone all over the town. (children put their arms over their heads
  for the sun)

  And then the grass began to grow,

  It grew all over the town, town, town.

  It grew all over the town. (children crouch down and
  pretend to grow)

  And then the flowers began to bloom,

  They bloomed all over the town, town, town.

  They bloomed all over the town. (children pretend to bloom like
  flowers)

Star Poems

Teaches About Stars

- These three poems teach about the wonderful stars.

  Higher than a house,

  Higher than a tree,

  Oh, whatever can that be?

  Starlight, star bright,

  First star I see tonight.

  I wish I may, I wish I might,

  Have the wish I wish tonight.

I saw a star slide down the sky,

Blinding the north as it went by.

Too lovely to be bought or sold,

Too burning and too quick to hold.

Good only to make wishes on,

And then forever to be gone.

Rain Poem

Practices Memory Skills

- This popular poem lends itself to practicing memory skills and experiencing language.

    Rain on the green grass,

    Rain on the trees,

    Rain on the rooftops,

    But not on me.

- Let the children name three things on which it rains, for example, sidewalk, kitten and windows.
- Repeat the poem, inserting these three things.

    Rain on the sidewalk,

    Rain on the kitten,

    Rain on the windows,

    But not on me.

- Always end with "But not on me."
- This game can get pretty silly.

Swimming in the Pool

Practices Rhyming Skills

- Recite this poem, letting the children fill in the rhyming word.

    When it's so hot,

    I like to get cool.

    I like to splash around

    In the swimming _____. (pool)

    I swim around,

Weather Games

And I make a wish.
I like to pretend
That I'm a _____. (fish)

So when it's hot,
Go and get cool.
Everybody swim
In the swimming _____. (pool)

By Jackie Silberg

Sea Shells

Improves Memory Skills

- Recite this poem with the children.

    Sea shells, sea shells,
    Some are rough and some are shiny.
    Sea shells, sea shells,
    Some are big and some are tiny.

    Shells are long,
    And shells are round.
    Shells can make an ocean sound.
    Whoosh, whoosh, whoosh. (make your voice sound like the
        swishing of waves)

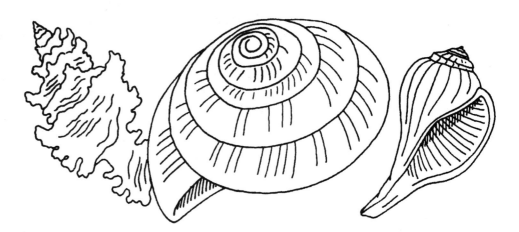

Weather Games

Goodbye, Summer

Teaches About Summer

- Sing to the tune of "Goodnight, Ladies."

  Goodbye, summer, goodbye, summer,

  Goodbye, summer,

  We're sad to see you go.
- Talk about what the children did during the summer, and why they are sad to say goodbye.
- Sing about those things.

  Goodbye, baseball...

  Goodbye, swimming...

  Goodbye, camping...

Thunderstorm Talk

Builds Weather Vocabulary

- While watching a thunderstorm, talk about the rain, the clouds and the smells of this weather condition.
- Ask the children where they think animals go for protection against the rain. Where do birds go? Where do rabbits and squirrels go?
- Ask the children what they like to do when it's raining.

Weather Games

The Seasons

- Recite the following poem and ask the children to name all the things that they can do during the different seasons.

  What can you do in the wintertime, wintertime, wintertime?

  What can you do in the wintertime,

  In the wintertime of the year?

- Each season will bring forth new vocabulary words.
- The wintertime might elicit responses such as ride sleds, ice skate, etc.
- Vocabulary for other seasons includes:

  Springtime—planting seeds, picking flowers

  Summertime—drinking lemonade, swimming

  Autumn time—raking leaves, carving pumpkins

Snow Words

- Find magazine pictures of snow scenes to show the children.
- Talk about compound words that include "snow": snowman, snowball, snowshoe, snowfall, etc.
- See if the children can add any words to the list.
- Look at the pictures to see if they show any of these "snow words."

Nine Little Reindeer

Develops Counting Skills

- During the winter, especially around Christmas time, children love acting out this poem.

  Peeking through the window, what do I see?
    (cup hands in front of eyes to peek)

  One little, two little, three little reindeer.
    (raise one finger for each number)

  Skipping through the sky with a clickety click,

  Four little, five little, six little reindeer.
    (raise one finger for each number)

  Better go to bed,

  Better close my eyes, (close eyes)

  If I want a big surprise!

  Listen to the rooftop,

  What do I hear? (put hands to ears to listen)

  Seven little, eight little, nine little, ten little reindeer.
    (raise one finger for each number)

  By Jackie Silberg

Winter Is Coming

Teaches About The Seasons

- This is a wonderful poem about how animals prepare for winter.

  Into their hive the busy bees crawl.
    (make your fingers walk)

  Into the anthills go ants one and all.

  The brown caterpillars have hidden their heads,
    (put one fist under the other fist)

  They spin silk cocoons for their snug little beds.

  The squirrels have gone into their holes in the trees.
    (put your arms behind your back)

  The bird nests are empty. No birds do we see.

  The elves have all gone for the winter, we know,

  There isn't a person who knows where they go.

Weather Games

Once There Was a Snowman

- This poem teaches children what happens to snow when the temperature rises.

    Once there was a snowman,

    Who stood outside my door.

    He thought he'd like to come inside,

    And run around the floor.

    He thought he'd like to warm himself,

    By the fireside red.

    He thought he'd like to climb upon,

    My big white bed.

    He called to the North Wind,

    "Help me now, I pray,

    I'm completely frozen,

    Standing here all day."

    So the North Wind came along,

    And blew him in the door.

    And now there's nothing left of him,

    But a puddle on the floor.

The Snowman

- Ask the children to pretend to be snowmen, first by growing tall and then by slowly melting.

    I made a little snowman,

    I made him big and round.

    I made him from a snowball,

    I rolled upon the ground.

    He has two eyes, a nose, a mouth,

    A lovely scarf of red.

    He even has some buttons,

    And a hat upon his head.

    Melt, melt, melt, melt,

    Melt, melt, melt, melt.

C-C-C-C-Cold

Develops Weather Vocabulary

- Recite the following call and response chant.
- When the children say the c-c-c-c-cold line, they cross their arms over their chests and pretend to shiver.

  There was a man and he did sing,

  C-c-c-c-c-c-cold.

  Across the north land it would ring,

  C-c-c-c-c-c-cold.

  No matter what he tried to say,

  C-c-c-c-c-c-cold.

  His words kept coming out this way,

  C-c-c-c-c-c-cold.

- This song is an excellent introduction to a discussion of proper clothing for cold weather.

Skills Index

Skills Index

Skills Index

Skills Index

Skills Index

Skills Index

Terms Index

Terms Index

Terms Index